REFLECTING THE IMAGE

*Our Call to Mirror
Christ to the World*

CARLA D. SUNBERG with KERI MITCHELL

BEACON HILL PRESS
OF KANSAS CITY

Beacon Hill Press of Kansas City
PO Box 419527
Kansas City, MO 64141
www.BeaconHillBooks.com

ISBN 978-0-8341-3527-7

Printed in the
United States of America

Cover Design: Sherwin Schwartzrock
Interior Design: Sharon Page

Library of Congress Cataloging-in-Publication Data
Sunberg, Carla D.
  Reflecting the image : our call to mirror Christ to the world / Carla D. Sunberg, with Keri Mitchell.
    pages cm
  Includes bibliographical references.
  ISBN 978-0-8341-3527-7 (pbk.)
  1. Jesus Christ—Example. 2. Image of God. 3. Mirrors—Religious aspects.
4. Imitation—Religious aspects—Christianity. 5. Christian life. I. Title.
  BT304.2.S86 2015
  233'.5—dc23
                                                          2015020104

10 9 8 7 6 5 4 3 2 1

CONTENTS

Dedicated to my precious family,
Chuck, Christy, and Cara,
who have embodied reflecting the Image!

A NEW-OLD UNDERSTANDING OF HOLINESS

Growing up in the holiness tradition, I used to think that holiness was all up to me: my choices, my behavior, my thoughts. To be the person God wanted me to be meant that I needed to follow a list of dos and don'ts to the best of my ability. I tried to live this way—and I failed.

A number of years ago, while on my spiritual journey, I began to learn something that changed my life: Holiness is not about us. It's all about Christ. He is *the* living and embodied Image of our very holy God, and every single human being is called to be a reflection of Jesus Christ in this world. His very nature screams holiness, and to be a holy people, we need to turn toward him and reflect his image.

This understanding came more and more into focus as I worked on my doctoral dissertation. We had spent thirteen years in Russia as missionaries, and throughout this time, I had to study the history of the Eastern church, because that was the context in which I served. I discovered that this part of Christianity is quite unfamiliar to much of the Western church. However, I also learned that John Wesley, the father of Methodism, had studied the early church fathers and that they had influenced his understanding of holiness. This led me to study some of the most influential individuals in Eastern church history, the fourth-century Cappadocian Fathers and the women related to them, women I've chosen to call the Cappadocian Mothers. My own reading of these individuals is informed by my Wesleyan heritage, and so I read them through that lens. At the same time, hidden in the pages of history, they taught me a great deal about the optimism that humanity can be restored in the image of God. Over and again they used "mirror imagery" in their teachings about what it means to be growing as a Christian and, specifically, in our relationship with Jesus Christ.

These days, it seems we are trying to teach people "Christianity lite" with five-minute devotionals and podcasts on the go. We find it marketed and sold as fast-food religion. Although we are incredibly busy people, we can't have a relationship with God in that short amount of time. It won't happen.

In Fort Wayne, Indiana, where I pastored a church with my husband, Chuck, we had the opportunity to bring a number of new people to Christ, and part of discipling them was teaching them to be in the Word and prayer every day. We followed the daily Scripture readings prescribed by Rev. Wayne Cordeiro, author of *The Divine Mentor*. He encourages "sitting at the feet of the Savior" and emphasizes that this is the primary job we have as Christians. When Chuck and I moved to Ohio to be co-district superintendents of the East Ohio District of the Church of the Nazarene, I wanted to continue this discipleship. I felt God leading me to do this through a daily blog, telling me, "As a spiritual leader in the church, let people know you're spending time with me every day and making me a priority." So that's what I do—I spend time in the Word in the mornings, and I ask, "Lord, what do you want me to learn from this today?" And then I write.

The blog is titled "Reflecting the Image," a theme based on my doctoral dissertation and guided by Cordeiro's Scripture selections. This book conflates a number of these daily devotional writings to tell the story of how our lives can change when we begin to understand holiness differently.

It changed my life. I hope and pray that it changes yours too.

ONE

THE REDEMPTION OF TARNISHED MIRRORS AND LOST COINS

You wouldn't learn what I look like if you visit my blog. That's because my profile photo is not a picture of me but a work of art by the Italian Baroque painter Domenico Fetti. It depicts a woman searching for her lost coin, based on a parable Jesus tells:

Or what woman having ten silver coins, if she loses one of them, does not light a lamp, sweep the house, and search carefully until she finds it? When she has found it, she calls together her friends and neighbors, saying, "Rejoice with me, for I have found the coin that I had lost." (Luke 15:8-9)

In the fourth century, the Cappadocian Fathers likened the story of the lost coin to the loss of the image of God within humanity. They believed that because of sin, humanity had tarnished the reflection but that no human was so lost that the capacity to reflect God had been destroyed.

The coin is somewhere in the house. The ability to reflect God is still within us, somewhere. This is the grace of God, constantly reaching out to humanity. The woman had to search the house. We must be willing to search our own hearts. The woman knew that this was a most precious possession, so she searched intently and even asked others to help her. The loss of God's image in humanity is so great that it ought to be the passion of our hearts—that which is lost must be found!

The coin probably was buried under dirt in a corner somewhere, and when the woman found it, she and her friends rejoiced. The image of God may be dirty and beaten up by the lifestyle we have led, but God can restore the image in us, for this is the purpose for which we were created.

Then God said, "Let us make humankind in our image, according to our likeness." . . .

So God created humankind in his image,
in the image of God he created them;
male and female he created them.

God blessed them, and God said to them, "Be fruitful and multiply, and fill the earth and subdue it; and have dominion over the fish of the sea and over the birds of the air and over every living thing that moves upon the earth." . . . God saw everything that he had made, and indeed, it was very good. (Gen. 1:26a, 27-28, 31a)

In this scene from Genesis, we read about the first wedding, a party in paradise for Adam and Eve, who were created to be equal partners, together ruling over the earth. And at this wedding, God is celebrating. He rejoices when he creates humanity, for both male and female are created in his very image.

This first wedding foreshadows the wedding invitation that weaves throughout all of Scripture. Those who are reflecting the image are invited to the marriage supper of the Lamb—to be the very bride of Christ! The whole story from beginning to end is the story of an invitation to God's creation to be united with him. From Genesis to Revelation he is saying, come! We were created to be at the wedding! We are invited.

We have to ask ourselves, have we ever responded to the invitation? For you and for me, the invitation is to turn around and face in the direction of God, our Creator, and to be mirrors that reflect his image. This invitation has been sent out through the eons and continues to be sent out today, to all of us. We must be willing to take our dirty, cracked, and broken mirror and face it in the direction of our loving Creator. When we do, he cleans us up until we are shiny and new, and then we become a reflection of our Creator.

Even for the most unlovely, those who are covered with dirt and beaten up by life, the coin is still in the house. The capacity is in humanity, and God never, ever turns his back on humanity. As long as we turn around, we can reflect him.

In the late 1980s, Wanda came wandering into our church in Austin, Texas. She had strayed about as far away from God as you possibly could. She'd had a baby two years before while unmarried and since then had embraced a lifestyle that included partying and frequenting numerous bars to get drunk. When she stumbled into our church, it was because she knew her life was a mess, and she remembered attending a little holiness church as a girl.

I went to visit her and BJ, the woman she lived with, and wound up convincing Wanda to come with me to the district's women's retreat. That was an adventure. I put her in my room because I knew her story, and it turned out that the woman rooming with the pastor's wife had packed Jack Daniel's and drugs in her luggage. I caught her drunk and confronted her. "All right," she told me. "I'm ready to get rid of it all." So we poured her alcohol down the drain. Little by little, over the next number of years, Wanda cleaned up and one day had a transformational experience in her life when she was overcome by the Holy Spirit. She never went back to her old life. A few years later the Lord revealed to her that she was to marry a man in her church. She married him, and her son grew up as a Christian. Today she's involved in a large Pentecostal church in Florida and gives God all the credit for what happened in her life.

It's tempting for us as Christians to dismiss people like Wanda as hopeless, but her story reminds us that no one is beyond the reach of God's redemptive love. As Wanda turned around to face God, he healed her and restored her into his image. He can do the same for anyone.

Christ Is *the* Image

If we've been in church long enough, we've heard the Christmas story and the Easter story and all of the Jesus stories in between hundreds of times. Perhaps somewhere along the way, the reality that God came to Earth to live among us, to be *with* us, has lost some of its wonder.

I always loved my childhood Christmases in Germany. Instead of Santa Claus, Saint Nicholas paid a visit to our home in early December and left either candy or coal in our shoes. None of us children ever received coal, though as a little girl, I used to think my brother Kurt ought to be given a few lumps of it. (Today Kurt and I are the best of friends, but when we were younger . . . oh my!)

Saint Nicholas, however, was not the big event—Christmas Eve was. We had an Advent calendar and opened one window every day, counting down to Christmas Eve, when we would worship at church. I remember the little German poem we would recite as we lit the candles in the Advent wreath. Translated to English, it says: "Advent, Advent, / A little candlelight burns. / First one, then two, then three, then four, / Then stands the Christ child before the door." When we arrived home from worship, the gifts were under the tree because the Christ child—the Gift—had arrived.

The excitement of Christmas was always about the coming of the Christ child. It wasn't about Santa Claus coming; he had already come, and he didn't bring the gifts. All he brought was chocolate. The German celebration of Christmas emphasized to me the real reason we celebrate—the incredible reality that God came in the flesh to minister to all of humanity.

Hebrews 1:3 says, "He is the reflection of God's glory and the exact imprint of God's very being, and he sustains all things by his powerful word. When he had made purification for sins, he sat down at the right hand of the Majesty on high." The "he" in this text refers to Jesus. From the onset of this epistle, the writer wants to make clear who Jesus is—God in the flesh. If we want to know what God looks like and acts like as a human being, we need only to look at Jesus, who is the "exact imprint of God's very being."

The implications of this for humanity are huge. Christ assumed human flesh, and in doing so, he healed human flesh. He set right the things that had gone wrong. The writer tells us that Jesus created a pathway for all of humanity to be "purified," or restored into the image of God. Everyone who seeks his face can be a reflection of Jesus to the world.

He is the image of the invisible God, the firstborn of all creation. . . . He is the head of the body, the church; he is the beginning, the firstborn from the dead, so that he might come to have first place in everything. For in him all the fullness of God was pleased to dwell, and through him God was pleased to reconcile to himself all things, whether on earth or in heaven, by making peace through the blood of his cross. (Col. 1:15, 18-20)

Here again, in this letter to the Colossians, the writer makes abundantly clear that Jesus Christ is the Image. God sent his Son to be the visible Image of the invisible God, and it is Christ's image that we are to be reflecting to the world around us. When we do, people see Jesus. As I read this passage of Scripture, the words "peace" and "reconciliation" resound in my ears. What would it be like if we, his "image bearers," were reflecting his peace and reconciliation to the world?

I remember a day my husband and I spent driving around east Ohio, making stops at different churches along the way. In a back "holler" near the Ohio River stands a beautiful church building that once upon a time was filled with worshippers. Today it has only a handful of members who can barely afford to keep the doors open. It's one of two churches in town, and both are suffering serious decline.

The community is depressed. The coal mines and steel mills have shut down. The latest census shows that 418 people are left in this town, and nearly everyone lives below the poverty level. Drug and alcohol abuse are rampant in this depressed part of the country. The entire community has become "unchurched." In an effort to reach out to children, the church held a weeklong vacation Bible school, and every evening only one child attended.

What people need is Christ! They need the living, incarnated Jesus Christ who can transform their lives. He is the solution to the problems that ail this little town in Ohio as well as the towns and cities across our country and throughout the world. So often these days, however, people say, "I want Jesus, but I don't want the church." So church members have to ask themselves, "How do we become Jesus to the communities around us?"

This is when things get personal. We have to take a long, hard look at our lives. If an entire church were made up of individuals who were a reflection of Jesus to the world, what would happen? Could we effectively minister to a community that has lost all hope? Isn't that what Jesus did when he entered this world, brought hope to a needy and dying world?

We are living in that needy and dying world today, and the hope, peace, and reconciliation of Jesus Christ found in the Image is what the world needs so desperately. Colossians 3:10 tells us we "have clothed" ourselves "with the new self, which is being renewed in knowledge according to the image of its creator." In other words, the Image is being renewed in us so that we look like him. It doesn't matter who we are; we can all be renewed into his image and then serve as a reflection of him to the world around us.

This is the call of the deeper walk with Jesus Christ—to be transformed into his image—so that as we walk this earth, people see Jesus in us and experience Christ, and hence God, here on earth.

The Image of a King Who Foreshadows the Image of the King

Since the dawn of creation, God has been reaching out to humanity, giving us glimpses of the Image. He is present in the opening chapters of the creation story, putting his imprint on all that we see around us. God is revealed in his relationship with Adam and Eve, Abraham and Moses. All of these are moments when God is breaking into human history.

There's an interesting little story in Genesis, not long before the destruction of Sodom and Gomorrah. The story of how God saves Lot and his family may be the one about Abraham's nephew that we know best, but it wasn't the first time God rescued Lot from Sodom.

Soon after God's call to Abram (before God renamed him Abraham) is a story of the kings of the region, who govern what appear to be little principalities. These kings make war against Sodom, and Lot and his family are taken away as plunder in that battle. When Abram learns of his nephew's fate, he leads the men of his household to pursue the kings and save Lot and his family. Though Abram was fighting against several kings, he was victorious. Genesis 14:16 says that Abram "brought back all the goods, and also brought back his nephew Lot with his goods, and the women and the people."

Then we meet Melchizedek, king of Salem.

After [Abram's] return from the defeat of Chedorlaomer and the kings who were with him, the king of Sodom went out to meet him at the Valley of Shaveh (that is, the King's Valley). And King Melchizedek of Salem brought out bread and wine; he was priest of God Most High. He blessed him and said,

"Blessed be Abram by God Most High,

maker of heaven and earth;

and blessed be God Most High,

who has delivered your enemies into your hand!"

And Abram gave him one-tenth of everything. Then the king of Sodom said to Abram, "Give me the persons, but take the goods for yourself." But Abram said to the king of Sodom, "I have sworn to the LORD, God Most High, maker of heaven and earth, that I would not take a thread or a sandal-thong or anything that is yours, so that you might not say, 'I have made Abram rich.' I will take nothing but what the young men have eaten, and the share of the men who went with me—Aner, Eshcol, and Mamre. Let them take their share." (Vv. 17-24)

Melchizedek is one of the "good" kings in the region and was not involved in the battle. He is identified here as a priest but appears in the Old Testament long before the line of Levi is established—the line from which all of the Israelite priests would later come. And he is not part of Abram's family, so he is not an Israelite; he's something completely other and different. Melchizedek comes from outside the structure.

God already has declared that he will make Abram the father of many nations, yet even Abram recognizes Melchizedek as a priest and worships God through this king of Salem by giving the king a tenth of all his plunder. Melchizedek was an earthly ambassador of God on high, and Abram, honoring him, gave him the tithe of victory.

Abram knew that he wanted God to have the credit for what had happened, and not human beings. This is found in his very purposeful response to the king of Sodom. Abram could have had considerable additional wealth as a result of the plunder from this altercation, but instead he refused to keep it and gave it back to the king of Sodom. He returned to the earth what was the earth's and gave in worship to God what was to be given to God—and God was given the glory for all that happened in his life!

Melchizedek's arrival on the scene was a completely countercultural event. Where in the world did he come from? Why is he serving the true God? We see him for a moment, and then he disappears again from the pages of history. It is almost as if the curtain is pulled back on the future, that he is a foreshadowing of the coming Messiah. The story of God's people is just beginning, and already this king begins a trajectory that will culminate in the life of Christ here on earth.

Melchizedek is king of Salem, which we know today as Jerusalem. Salem means "peace," which is symbolic. Could it be that he is laying the groundwork for the "Prince of Peace"? In his worship of God, Melchizedek broke the bread and shared the wine. Here, Abram was already partaking of a meal like that which would become, for all of time, the Lord's Supper.

We don't meet Melchizedek again in the Old Testament, but we revisit his story in the New Testament letter to the Hebrews:

Now if perfection had been attainable through the levitical priesthood—for the people received the law under this priesthood—what further need would there have been to speak of another priest arising according to the order of Melchizedek, rather than one according to the order of Aaron? For when there is a change in the priesthood, there is necessarily a change in the law as well. Now the one of whom these things are spoken belonged to another tribe, from which no one has ever served at the altar.

For it is evident that our Lord was descended from Judah, and in connection with that tribe Moses said nothing about priests.

It is even more obvious when another priest arises, resembling Melchizedek, one who has become a priest, not through a legal requirement concerning physical descent, but through the power of an indestructible life. For it is attested of him,

"You are a priest forever,

according to the order of Melchizedek." (7:11-17)

We don't know who wrote the letter to the Hebrews, but we know that the author is writing to the Jews. The writer is telling us that when Jesus came, he was remembered as being a priest forever in "the order of Melchizedek."

This is significant because Melchizedek came from outside the order, superseding the whole system of the Jews. There was no need for the priests of Levi. Somehow Abram understood that Melchizedek was special and unique, and he responded to the ministry of this king. Abram's response to him shows us the importance of our response to the Messiah.

Jesus, like Melchizedek, was completely "other." He came from outside the system to establish a new system, a new covenant that went beyond the bounds of the traditional religious practices of the day. It was a frustration to the religious leaders, but this had been God's plan for centuries. He knew that this was what would need to happen to be able to set people free. The Levitical priests always had to make sacrifices for themselves, but Christ is the sacrifice for all, breaking the order of the Levites. And it's not just about that sacrifice; it's following after something completely new and different. Jesus came to earth, and his life, death, and resurrection changed the whole system.

What's exciting about Melchizedek's story is that this Old Testament king reveals a moment when God steps into history and nudges humanity in the right direction. Melchizedek is a foreshadowing of Christ, a visible image of God. God so wants to reconcile humanity to himself that he is already revealing a glimpse of his image in this odd Old Testament story.

Abraham is the father of our faith, and for the Jews reading the letter to the Hebrews, no one on earth was more revered. So if Abraham worshipped God through Melchizedek, then this superseded the Levitical system of priests and sacrifices. Jesus was in the order of Melchizedek. It's a new order. It's a new day.

There are moments in our lives today when we have experiences that foreshadow what lies ahead. What are we responding to and seeing these days? Our lives are also to be a foreshadowing of Christ, for his image is stamped on us. The world is hungry for Christians whom it can truly respect. This is a humbling message, because it was not often that there were faithful individuals, like Melchizedek, who broke into time and space for the world to see the coming Messiah. The challenge is to live each and every day in the grace of God, allowing his image to be brought into clearer focus so that our lives touch the world and give a momentary glimpse of what is to come.

Discussion Questions

1. Do you know anyone who epitomizes the lost coin, someone who seems too buried in sin to be found by God? Have you ever felt like a lost coin?

2. Genesis talks about us being created in the "image of God." In the light of this chapter, what does that mean?

3. What is your response when you think of God coming to Earth and putting on human flesh to be with us?

4. What do people mean when they say, "I want Jesus, but I don't want the church"?

5. What about Melchizedek's story stands out to you?

6. Can you think of a time that God has broken into your life to reveal himself? Perhaps through someone else who is reflecting God's image?

TWO

WHAT ARE OUR MIRRORS REFLECTING?

I spent eight years of my childhood in Frankfurt, where my father pastored a church. My parents were missionaries, and though we lived near a US military base and went to school with other American children, my parents determined that we would immerse ourselves in the German language and culture. My three older brothers and I learned German and made lots of German friends, as well as American ones.

My three big brothers were always up to something and had an entire gang of neighborhood friends who would join in the "some-things" of the day. When Halloween rolled around, my brothers—who knew where all the Americans lived—taught their German friends how to say "trick or treat" and took them door-to-door. The German kids came home with bags of American candy and thought it was the most awesome thing!

As pastor's kids, we figured we had free rein of the church. It was not a small building, and I remember one sunny day my brothers and their friends got a hold of a large full-length mirror and took it all the way up to the roof of the church. (Looking back, this was probably not a very smart thing to do, but they were the cool teenagers, so I wasn't going to protest!) The boys wanted to see what would happen if they used that mirror to reflect the light of the sun in different directions. How far away could they see that reflection?

Imagine their delight as they reflected this bright light blocks away—and into the windows of unsuspecting neighbors. Our parsonage near the church was one of the few houses around; most of our neighbors lived in apartments, so a good number of people were enlightened, so to speak, by the boys' scientific experiment! In a very small way they had harnessed the light of the sun, even if only in its reflection.

What would happen if God's children grabbed their mirrors, climbed up to the very highest point, and aimed in his direction? The people of the world would be blinded by what they saw, for they would experience heaven on earth.

You and I were created as mirror images of God. And as Scripture shows us time and again, God continually breaks through history to reveal his image to humanity, ultimately sending his Son to earth in the flesh to become *the* Image of God. We are invited into a deeply personal relationship with Jesus Christ, a relationship in which we are challenged to harness the reflection of the Son and shine him into the dark and unsuspecting corners of our world.

The Image is always in close proximity to us. All we have to do is turn and face Jesus. But we also can choose to turn our backs, and when we do, our lives become a reflection of the world.

Claiming to be wise, they became fools; and they exchanged the glory of the immortal God for images resembling a mortal human being or birds or four-footed animals or reptiles.

Therefore God gave them up in the lusts of their hearts to impurity, to the degrading of their bodies among themselves, because they exchanged the truth about God for a lie and worshiped and served the creature rather than the Creator, who is blessed forever! Amen. (Rom. 1:22-25)

Here, in his letter to the Romans, Paul is describing the fall of humanity. Humans were created to be a reflection of the Image! However, once we turned our backs on God, we could no longer reflect him because we were no longer facing him. Rather than reflecting his image, we were reflecting the world around us. Instead of being mirror images of an incorruptible God, we were mirroring the images of corruptible humanity and even the behaviors of the creatures of this earth. Humans chose to worship and serve the creatures rather than the very Creator himself. We were reflecting ourselves!

Paul's indictment against humanity is applicable to us today. We are to be his image bearers, but we have turned our backs on him. Even followers of Jesus Christ follow him at a distance—and with so much distance between him and our mirrors, our reflection of the Image is so small that it is barely visible.

The ugliness of this world is being reflected in those who profess to follow Christ. We are enticed by the things of this world. We want to look like the people of this world. We want to have the things the world has to offer. And the worst is that in our relationships, we have given up the things of God to behave in a creaturely fashion. We even have adopted animal-like behaviors in some instances, following instincts that lead us into activities that are not pleasing to God. Many of these activities can result in addictions that we find terribly difficult to break. The world tells us that these things are acceptable, so we make no effort to change.

They Gave Up Their Mirrors

Exodus 38:8 says, "He made the basin of bronze with its stand of bronze, from the mirrors of the women who served at the entrance to the tent of meeting." We can learn a lot from this one little verse. At this point in their history, the Israelites are wandering in the wilderness, not that far removed from Egypt. They had lived among the Egyptians for many generations and were deeply influenced by their practices. Even after they experienced the glory of God in the parting of the Red Sea, in the pillars of cloud and fire, and in the manna from heaven, they still refused to give up some of their Egyptian ways.

The custom of Egyptian women was to take their mirrors with them when they went to worship their gods. Mirrors often were flattened plates of bronze or another metal that had been polished into a reflective sheen. The mirrors were held in wood frames or hung on a cord around the neck of a woman, as a necklace. The reason she carried her mirror with her to the temples was so she could stop and fix herself up before going inside. She was concerned with her appearance and wanted to ensure that she was properly attired and made up before attending to worship so she could please the gods and, presumably, impress fellow worshippers as well. This is what the Israelite women had learned from the Egyptians, as their slaves.

But now the Israelites have been delivered from Egypt, and it was time to build the tabernacle, the place where the people of God could worship him. The instructions had been given, and the construction was ongoing. Whenever there was a need for more material, the Israelites had given of their belongings to meet the need. This time, it was the Israelite women who stepped up to the task.

Before the tabernacle was finished, Moses pitched a tent outside the Israelites' camp, and it was there that God met with him. This was holy ground, and the Israelite women were the keepers of the door. People probably camped around the Tent of Meeting waiting to hear what it was God had to say. Perhaps the women kept the area clean and might have cooked meals for Moses. They likely guarded the door at all hours, making sure no one snuck in. I imagine a number of women worked in this position, taking shifts at different times. We don't know whether they were assigned to do this or did this out of a sense of duty, but it was a position of responsibility.

Yet while they were caring for the entrance to the meeting place of God, the Israelite women still wore a symbol of Egyptian worship. As they began to understand the importance of their role in the worship of the one true God, they realized they needed to take their eyes off themselves and look to God. Over and over in the Old Testament, we are reminded to seek the face of God. Why is that? So that we will be drawn toward the Image. It's hard to seek the face of God, however, when we are wearing mirrors around our necks that encourage us to constantly seek our own faces!

The women finally, and willingly, gave up their mirrors, letting them be melted so they could be used to make the basin of bronze, along with its stand, for the tabernacle of God. This was not just a practical matter but spoke volumes about the women's understanding of their relationship with God. The very item that symbolized self-centeredness for the Israelite women was given up to be used in the heart of the worship experience for the whole community.

Don't we behave as the Israelites in our Christian lives too? We worship and serve God but still carry our self-centeredness with us. What would that symbol of self-centeredness be for us today? Is it the style of music we want to experience in the worship service? The way the minister dresses? The length of the sermon?

How many people today shop around for just the right church for them? *For them?* Isn't church about God? At least it should be about God, but we have made it all about us and what it is that *we* want.

The women who served at the entrance to the Tent of Meeting had a spiritual encounter. I imagine that while serving where God made himself present, they experienced something of the overflow of his presence. In response, they became willing to stop primping and worrying about themselves when they went to worship. It was no longer about how they liked it or what they wanted; it was about God and him alone.

Their mirrors were reflecting themselves, and they had to give them up so they could truly serve God. We must do the same. Are we willing to give up our mirrors?

Smoke and Mirrors

Perhaps our mirrors are reflecting ourselves. Perhaps they are reflecting other idols—people or objects we worship in place of God. We were created to reflect the Image, but in sin we can choose to face the other direction and reflect something or someone else.

When they had gone through the whole island as far as Paphos, they met a certain magician, a Jewish false prophet, named Bar-Jesus. He was with the proconsul, Sergius Paulus, an intelligent man, who summoned Barnabas and Saul and wanted to hear the word of God. But the magician Elymas (for that is the translation of his name) opposed them and tried to turn the proconsul away from the faith. But Saul, also known as Paul, filled with the Holy Spirit, looked intently at him and said, "You son of the devil, you enemy of all righteousness, full of all deceit and villainy, will you not stop making crooked the straight paths of the Lord? And now listen—the hand of the Lord is against you, and you will be blind for a while, unable to see the sun." Immediately mist and darkness came over him, and he went about groping for someone to lead him by the hand. When the proconsul saw what had happened, he believed, for he was astonished at the teaching about the Lord. . . .

. . . When the meeting of the synagogue broke up, many Jews and devout converts to Judaism followed Paul and Barnabas, who spoke to them and urged them to continue in the grace of God.

The next sabbath almost the whole city gathered to hear the word of the Lord. But when the Jews saw the crowds, they were filled with jealousy; and blaspheming, they contradicted what was spoken by Paul. (Acts 13:6-12, 43-45)

These stories took place when Paul and Barnabas were out on their missionary journey sharing the good news with anyone who would listen. What they ran into were people motivated by their own selfish greed, worshipping—and thereby reflecting—themselves and encouraging others to follow them instead of Christ.

The missionaries first sailed to the island of Paphos, where they ran into a sorcerer who was using magic tricks to lead people astray. There was no encouragement to follow God, but to follow him. His motivation was personal gain, not the spiritual lives of the people within his community. Paul was able to look him in the eye and see him for who he truly was.

Next they found a deterrent to their ministry in the form of good religious folk. Paul and Barnabas visited in Pisidian Antioch and preached the fulfillment of the Old Testament prophecies. This was what everyone had been waiting for. With great excitement, the people packed the synagogue to capacity on the second Sabbath that Paul and Barnabas were there. On the first Sabbath, the religious officials were excited about the truth they were hearing—about the fulfillment of all that they had been waiting for—but by the second Sabbath, they were filled with jealousy. Their motivation to be popular outweighed even the good news. They were willing to distort the truth to retain power and favor among the people.

Oh, the draw of power! Most of us live our lives without much power. We are the simple and ordinary people of this world—and yet give us just a little power, and who knows what we might do with it?

During the days of the Soviet Union, fuel for cars often was in short supply because the delivery system was ineffective. Gas stations were too few, and they weren't run efficiently. Almost every station was run by a woman who became known as the "Gas Queen" because of the power she exerted over the fuel supply. She was to take the money and turn on the pump, but what power is contained in that simple act! Even a poor and uneducated woman could exert her influence within her community. She could choose to shut down the station for an extended lunch break. People would then be forced to line up outside her station for an hour waiting for her to finish her cup of tea. She could choose to allow you only a few liters of fuel instead of filling up your tank. Bribes were always welcome. An extra tip for her and her family might garner you the ability to fill your tank to the top. You had to be nice to the "Gas Queen" or you would be without fuel for your vehicle. Her motivation was not to help out those around her but to get the most that she could out of what she could control.

You would think that if someone had the best news for all of humanity, we would do anything that we could to share it with the world. Sadly, that is not the case. There are those like the "Gas Queen," who want to control the flow. They want to let it out when they have gotten enough for themselves. The world today also is filled with sorcerers. There are those who are willing to do magic tricks for earthly gain. Maybe it's for the money, but maybe it's for the power.

Years ago a popular preacher known for massive healings came to our city. Interestingly, workers were assigned to the doors to screen people before they were allowed to attend. My husband and one of our coworkers were curious and wanted to see what these services were really like. But when they arrived at the arena, because they were ministers, they were not allowed inside. The door attendants told them there was no room left, but they could tell that this was a lie. The "ministry" simply didn't want them to scrutinize what was (and wasn't) going on inside.

Paul looked the sorcerer right in the eye and saw that he was evil. There are times when we need to look evil right in the eye and call it out for what it is, for there are too many who are trying to deceive the people of God. There is obviously no reflection of Christ in these individuals.

But what about the good religious folks who at first believed and then argued against Paul and Barnabas? Look out for when God pours out his Holy Spirit. When there is a spirit of revival, there will be those who will speak against it. We must ask God for discernment in the midst of revival. We need to make sure this is his movement—but when it *is* his movement, he gets the credit, and the manifestations will be in line with the workings of Jesus Christ.

If we are a reflection of Christ, then the things that we do will look like Christ. A reflection cannot do anything that the original does not. When a preacher begins to do things that Jesus never would have done, we need to ask ourselves whether this is truth. How could it be when the call of the Christian life is radical transformation into the image of Christ? If the preacher or the teacher doesn't look or act like Christ—run! May God help us to be his discerning followers in an age when the truth about Jesus is desperately needed.

Following Christ or Following Customs?

We ourselves are Jews by birth and not Gentile sinners; yet we know that a person is justified not by the works of the law but through faith in Jesus Christ. And we have come to believe in Christ Jesus, so that we might be justified by faith in Christ, and not by doing the works of the law, because no one will be justified by the works of the law. But if, in our effort to be justified in Christ, we ourselves have been found to be sinners, is Christ then a servant of sin? Certainly not! But if I build up again the very things that I once tore down, then I demonstrate that I am a transgressor. For through the law I died to the law, so that I might live to God. I have been crucified with Christ; and it is no longer I who live, but it is Christ who lives in me. And the life I now live in the flesh I live by faith in the Son of God, who loved me and gave himself for me. (Gal. 2:15-20)

There was a great struggle in the early church over the rules. Whose rules were Christians going to follow? Peter and Paul, both Jews by birth, had disagreements about how to relate to the Gentiles, who were being addressed in this letter from Paul. Peter initially had thought that they would need to become like the Jews, and we know that's in the background as Paul writes. The two men had been raised in very different ways, and their perspectives on the Christian life were different. They both had to really dig down deep and ask themselves whether they were following Christ or customs. Sometimes it's hard for folks to distinguish between the two because they allow them to become so intertwined. The result in this case was that people were being caught up in the law, and it was clouding their ability to truly see Christ.

In the church today, just as in the time of Peter and Paul, we sometimes allow customs to cloud our mirrors. It's so easy for us to get caught up in "the way we've always done it." When my family lived in Russia as missionaries, our worship services took place in a horse stable that had been used for the equestrian events during the 1980 Olympics. Horses were stabled right down the hall, and cats ran through the aisles. It was stinky and dirty. This was on my mind the Sunday morning we prepared for our first baptism in our Russian church. My eyes alighted on a white afghan on the couch in our apartment, and I grabbed it so we would have something to put on the filthy floor for kneeling. I also picked up a crystal bowl thinking we could use it to hold the water that we would sprinkle on those being baptized. (Immersion wasn't an option for us, unless we wanted to use a horse trough.)

The next time we celebrated a baptism, I grabbed the afghan and crystal bowl again, thinking that they worked well the last time. By that time we understood more of the Russian language, and we overheard our congregants talking to each other about the symbol-ism of the white afghan and the crystal bowl and how this was the way baptism should be done. A couple of objects that had been no more than convenient already had turned into a sacred custom, and I thought, "Oh my, what have we done?"

We had been warned while training as missionaries that when you start a new ministry, people think everything you do is a tradi-tion and always has to be done that way. That hadn't dawned on us until the baptisms. It was akin to that story about the family who insisted on trimming the ends of the ham for Easter dinner because that's how Grandma had done it. Then one Easter, Grandma noticed and asked why the ends were being trimmed. When the family told her they were simply following her recipe, she explained, "I cut off the ends because my pan was too small."

There can be great value and meaning in church traditions, but sometimes we continue traditions simply for the sake of doing things "the way we've always done it" without any remembrance of why the customs began. Jesus knew this about us. Think about the different ways he performed miracles—spitting in the mud to heal the blind man one time, speaking words of healing the next. He healed people in different ways, which was incredibly intentional.

After overhearing the "symbolism" of the white afghan and the crystal bowl, we began performing baptisms at our youth center out-side the city, which had a nearby pond. We wanted to make sure our congregants knew it didn't have to be only one way. When we allow these customs to become law and supersede Christ, our mirrors will be clouded and the image of Christ will be distorted in our lives.

For Paul, in his letter to the Galatians, it was faith in Jesus Christ, not in the law, that would bring salvation. Paul realized that identi-fication with Christ and him alone is the core of the Christian faith. He no longer wanted to live for the law and instead wanted to live for God, declaring, "I have been crucified with Christ; and it is no longer I who live, but it is Christ who lives in me" (vv. 19-20).

Called to Be Icons

Stripping away the things of the world and placing our faith in Jesus Christ alone is pretty radical. Imagine the pressures the early apostles faced to live a certain way or to do certain things! They were rejected in many Jewish synagogues for preaching about Christ. The life and teachings of Jesus were more than most people could take. He sounded a little unbalanced! He wanted his followers to believe in a heavenly kingdom and stop concerning themselves with earthly kingdoms. He wanted them to serve the poor. He wanted them to peacefully respond when the world was fighting around them. He wanted them to love him and their neighbors above themselves. He wanted them to imitate him. He wanted them to be a reflection of him to the world each and every day.

Jesus' desire for his followers hasn't changed. If we were to strip away everything that we have placed on top of our understanding of Christianity and get down to Christ alone, what would our faith look like? Are we a reflection of Jesus to the world, or are we a reflection of our beliefs about Christ to the world? There is a big difference. Often we conjecture our own understandings about Christ. We think we are reflecting him, but actually we are reflecting a message to the world that is far different from the real Christ. Our reflection is clouded with the layers upon layers that we have created within the earthly community of faith. The sad truth is that this distortion may be even more dangerous than the outright wicked reflection. At least the wicked reflection is pretty obvious and we avoid it. The clouded reflection can be used to draw people away from the real Image.

Our world is hungry for Jesus. It wants and needs him desperately. But we are surrounded by images that distract us from the Image. Our world is filled with icons. One cultural icon of our day was Steve Jobs. In the last thirty years, this man has literally changed the planet in the way we live our lives. I am writing this on my iPad, and shortly I'll be using my iPhone to call my husband. My writing is saved somewhere in an iCloud, and I'm not sure what we would do without our iTunes. (They're pretty helpful in creating playlists for worship services.) Not only is Steve Jobs an icon, but he also reinserted the word "icon" into the vernacular. His company, Apple, created apps that can be activated by clicking on an "icon." Even non-Apple products, such as Androids, have copied the concept of the icon. (I imagine that this whole paragraph would have been like a foreign language just a few short years ago.)

Are there times when we worship the god of materialism? The gadgets of our day have come to fill our lives. They can do all kinds of tricks for us, and we enjoy them, but do we allow them to consume us? We are created to reflect the Image to a world that is dying and suffocating from all its stuff—the material things that will eventually suck the life out of us until we are left gasping for air.

But if people look at us, what do they see? Do they see the Image reflected in us, or do they see the icons of materialism?

Undoubtedly, icons have become a part of our lives. But icons have been in existence for hundreds of years, if not thousands. The early church developed icons as a way of passing the faith from one generation to the next. To this day, Orthodox churches are adorned with numerous icons, and each one has an "iconostasis," a wall separating the nave from the sanctuary with icons and religious paintings that tell the gospel story. (I like to tell people it's much like the flannel board that we used in Sunday school classes of the past, only much more expensive!)

Perhaps this religious tradition grew out of the practice of Roman emperors. The emperor wanted the people of his kingdom to know who he was; therefore he commissioned the finest masters in the known world to create paintings and sculptures, icons of himself to be placed throughout the kingdom. These were to be as real as possible, with one purpose in mind—someday, when one of his subjects saw the real emperor, they would know it was him because they had already seen the icon.

In the fourth century, Basil the Great spoke of this concept of the icon. He moved monasteries to the cities because he believed that God's people were to be icons to the world. Instead of living as hermits and pursuing the Christian life in solitude, Basil believed that the time within the monastery should be spent being molded and crafted by the finest workmen of the day, the monks' spiritual leaders. Then, as the monks grew in the spiritual life, they would become more and more perfect representations of the King. As they walked through the city streets and ministered to the poor and needy, the world would see Christ in action.

The world is in desperate need of real icons today, ones who will step out into the world and be Jesus. As followers of Jesus Christ, we are all called to be icons. This is the very root of the holiness message. By the power of the Holy Spirit, we are constantly, day in and day out, transformed into the image of Jesus Christ. We are to be icons of him as we step out into the world. Our world desperately needs schoolteachers who are icons, bandleaders who are icons, businesspeople who are icons, pastors who are icons, nurses who are icons, doctors who are icons, factory workers who are icons, lawyers who are icons.

What kind of icon are we? Are we reflecting the wrong image? It takes courage to admit that we have been facing the wrong direction. However, if we desire to turn around and seek his face, he will be there to help us. His grace will draw us into his presence, and we may again be restored to be his image bearers.

Discussion Questions

1. Can you think of a way in which God has broken into your own life to reveal his image?

2. Recalling what mirrors meant to the Israelite women, what are our symbols of self-centeredness today? How do we make church, worship, and God about us?

3. Generally, the areas of life that garner most of our attention and interest are the things that will be reflected in our lives. When people get to know you, what do they find out about you? Do they discover, for example, how many and what types of cars you own?

4. Have you ever questioned a spiritual leader or a movement for not looking or acting like Christ?

5. What customs of ours might cloud and distort the image of Christ?

6. Can you think of people who are true icons of Christ? Describe what makes them "iconic."

THREE

REFLECTING LOVE

Chapter 13 of Paul's first letter to the church in Corinth—commonly known as the "love chapter"—is one of the most well-known biblical texts, extending beyond the walls of the church. Officiants read it at weddings, crafters etch its words onto home décor, and greeting-card companies recognize it as a proven commodity. But we have super-spiritualized Corinth because we've taken these scriptures out of context. It's important for us to remember that Corinth was a problem church and to recognize that its problems were very similar to those we face today.

The city of Corinth lies at the bottom of a mountainous cliff, and on top of the mountain was a pagan temple. Because part of the worship of the people was sexual, the temple had more than one thousand prostitutes. They worked in shifts and would come down into the marketplace to solicit. When I visited Corinth, a tour guide told us that women actually carved the words "follow me" into the bottom of their sandals, stamping the words into the dirt to drum up business. As a result, sexually transmitted diseases ran rampant in this city. The people of Corinth believed in a god of healing and had plaster casts made of the body parts that needed healing to bring before that god. In a museum we visited, I was overwhelmed when I saw piles of plaster casts of human genitalia discovered in archaeological digs. The STDs must have been at almost epidemic levels.

This is the context into which Paul brings a church, and the problem in Corinth is that people keep bringing the world into the church with them. When he comments on the way women dress, for example (1 Cor. 11:4-7; see also 1 Tim. 2:9), his point is not that we should all look Amish; he is directly attacking them for dressing like the prostitutes. When he talks about the meat sacrificed to idols (1 Cor. 8:4-13; 10:25-31), he's addressing the disparity in the congregation between the really rich and the really poor.

Poor girls who had been temple prostitutes were coming to Christ, and if people were poor, it was cheaper to buy secondhand meat that had been used in sacrifice to the pagan gods. Then they would take it to the church potluck, and rich people would say they wouldn't eat it because of its pagan history, but it was the only thing the poor could afford. That's really what that whole issue was about. Or when Paul talks about not eating the Lord's Supper unworthily (11:27)—a passage we've kind of used to beat people down in the church—it's really a rich versus poor story. The Lord's Supper happened at the end of a potluck-type meal the church had together. Rich people showed up early in the day because they didn't have to work, and by the time poor people came, the food and wine, for both the meal and the Lord's Supper, were gone. So Paul suggested that everyone eat at home and then come to church and take part in the Lord's Supper together. He was talking to this community of faith about how to act like and be a community. How do you get together and have the Lord's Supper and disregard the people in your community who are starving by eating up all the food before they get there? Obviously, it's not just about taking Communion. Paul told them to treat their poor brothers and sisters with the same love and respect as they did those who had wealth.

Corinth also is on a strange little isthmus, and travelers from the west had to pass through it as they journeyed to Greece, Turkey, or Ephesus, so it became a huge crossroads for humanity where people spoke many different languages. When Paul is talking about languages and gifts (chap. 12), he is likely addressing people who were braggarts about their multilingual abilities. Paul himself spoke several languages, but he warns the church in Corinth that the gift of tongues can be divisive. At the end of the day, he wants them to understand what unites them.

I've been to Corinth a couple of times, and it's amazing how suddenly your perspective changes, and you begin to realize these people lived in a very modern world. It's rich. It's poor. It's a wild town with a wild history, with some people made homeless in their own hometown. At one time, it was estimated that two hundred thousand people lived on this one little isthmus. Can you imagine how bad the air would have been if everybody had his or her own fire going? It was a metropolitan area with all kinds of issues—a lot like those we face today. People who lived in Corinth weren't willing to give up the things of the world and their customs, both Jewish and pagan. It's so problematic that Paul wrote four letters to this church; two of them made it into our canon of Scriptures.

In his first letter, as he addresses all of the problems that divide the church, Paul leads the people to the climactic moment: he tells them that there is nothing greater than love—because love is God and God is love. This is so profound that Paul wants his followers to understand that everything else they fuss or argue over is nothing compared to participating in God through Christ and allowing his love to transform them into his holy people. The depths of this love are beyond our comprehension, for Paul is talking about the very nature of the triune God whom we worship.

When we talk about the love of God, we are talking about the Trinity. God is relationship. God is community. God the Father loves the Son, who loves the Spirit, and so on. In this relationship, we see mutual reciprocation and submission, an intermingling of hearts. And God asks us to be a reflection of this Trinitarian love.

Sadly, we have misconstrued what Paul means in 1 Corinthians 13 when he talks about love. We have this human understanding of love—this do-good, feel-good, let-everybody-do-what-they-want kind of "luv." My husband likes to call it, "I *luv* my truck" love. This is the world's understanding, and we have let it seep into our own understanding. But that is *not* what Paul is talking about. God's love is much different from having a warm, fuzzy feeling about a truck. Later Peter tells these new Christ followers, and us as well, that we are to participate in the divine nature of holy love. This is a love so pure and powerful that it makes all the arguments of this world pale in comparison. If God's nature is love, there is nothing else!

Are We the Dim Mirrors?

Paul understood, however, the limitations of our spiritual journey while here in the flesh. He says that while we live here on this earth we only see God dimly, as if through a mirror (1 Cor. 13:12). That is, we are unable at this time to see him face-to-face. We are able to participate in God, but from a distance. We are able to experience his nature—his holy love—but again, only from a distance.

The mirrors in the time of Paul were made of polished metal, probably bronze, like the mirrors used by the Israelite women at the Tent of Meeting. So they were not as clear as our modern mirrors. Reflected images were not distorted, but they were somewhat dim. This is the way in which we are able to see our Lord now, and thus we can know only "in part" (v. 12), anticipating the day when we will see him face-to-face and our knowledge of him will be total and complete.

Here is the beauty: We *can* know his nature now, and we can begin to taste what it will be like when we will know God fully. And that little bit of a foretaste is what Paul tries to capture in this chapter, for God's nature is pure, holy love. We should seek his face, spend time with him, and unite with him until we can see him face-to-face. When we do this, we allow his love to flow into our hearts and lives, then flow out of us as we interact with the world.

I'm wondering, too, if we might be seeing something in this word from Paul about reflecting the Image to the world, and not just about us seeing the Image. Let's step back a moment.

Paul is calling the people of Corinth into a deeper walk and relationship with Jesus Christ. The people in the church have become hung up on spiritual gifts and fighting over who is better, more powerful, or more significant. This is a *huge* problem because when the world looks at the church, it is not supposed to see a group of individuals trying to show off their own spiritual gifts; it is supposed to see Jesus. How does the world see Jesus in the midst of church folk? When those people are a reflection of Jesus Christ in the world. We are called to reflect the Image. Could it be that Paul is referring to the spiritual state of the Corinthians in this verse—the fact that both he and the world around them were seeing only a dim reflection of the Image because the Corinthians themselves were not the best reflection of Christ? Could it be that they were the dim mirrors?

Until Jesus comes again, the only reflection of Jesus that the world will see is the one in you and me. If the world is seeing only a dim reflection of Jesus, it's not Jesus' fault—it's yours and mine.

When people say that there doesn't seem to be much activity of the Holy Spirit in our world or in our churches these days, it means that there isn't much reflection of Jesus happening in our midst. Paul knew that it would take time in prayer and in seeking the face of God for our reflection to become clearer. Our intimate knowledge of Jesus Christ would grow as we draw closer and closer to him. And the closer we are to him, the clearer the reflection of Jesus will be in our lives. And the clearer the reflection of Jesus in you and in me, the more the world will be blessed by the reflection of the Image in its midst.

Living in Communion with Our Creator

How do we get there? By falling deeply in love with Jesus. We've missed this! We're so caught up in Corinthianesque arguments about eating and drinking and living that we've forgotten we are supposed to fall in love with Jesus. This conjures up romantic notions that may make us uncomfortable, but think about new Christians and the emotions they often experience when finding themselves in Jesus' embrace for the first time.

The imagery in Song of Solomon contains this kind of romantic language between the bridegroom and his bride. The picture of the lover and his "beloved" is one of an incredibly intimate relationship, and sometimes the descriptions make us blush. However, this picture of human love and intimacy reveals God's unfathomable love for us, which is waiting to be poured out. God wants us to be his beloved, and as his beloved, we will be loved and cared for by him.

How does the Bible begin? With a wedding. And how does it end? With the marriage supper of the Lamb. Right in the middle is Song of Solomon, and this is no accident. At the Council of Jamnia, Rabbi Aqiba stated, "The whole world is not worth the day on which the Song of Songs was given to Israel, for all the Scriptures are holy, but the Song of Songs is the Holy of Holies."[1] We find Song of Solomon halfway through the journey of Scripture, reminding us that we should be working toward this kind of intimacy with Christ—falling in love with him, uniting with him, just as in a marriage. We are to become the bride of Christ. This is an entirely different understanding from that of merely following a set of rules.

He brought me to the banqueting house, and his intention toward me was love. (Song of Sol. 2:4, NRSV)

Let him lead me to the banquet hall, and let his banner over me be love. (2:4, NIV)

God, through his prevenient grace, is constantly reaching out to all of humanity, drawing us toward him. He is the one who invites us—the body of Christ, the bride—to his banqueting table. The banqueting hall or banqueting table is where the bread and wine were served at a wedding. It was typical for those who served in the military to carry banners that proclaimed their strength and prowess. The banner of the leader would be placed at the entrance to a banqueting hall, extolling the abilities of this leader to all who entered. But our Bridegroom, instead of trying to intimidate us with his formidable power, drapes a banner of love over us. The *New International Version* identifies the very nature of the One who has brought us to the table. He is love! God is love! At the same time the *New Revised Standard Version* tells us "his intention toward" us is "love."

Notice also the differences in verb tense in these translations. Part of the reason for this is that English becomes limiting, but if we put the two translations together, we get a sense that God has been leading and also is continuing to lead us to his banqueting table. It is an ongoing action. The eternal God persistently reaches out to all of humanity and pours out his love on us, wanting to bring us to a place of intimacy in our relationship with him.

Remember that song from camp and vacation Bible school, "His Banner over Me Is Love"? I think about how many times I must have sung that song, motions and all, but I don't really think I knew what I was singing about. I'm glad that it's one of those that sticks in your mind, because when I begin to think about the incredible love of God that awaits us at his banqueting table, I am simply overwhelmed. It's not just a fun camp song! God, in his powerful love, is ushering us into his very presence. He doesn't want to strong-arm us but wants to woo us, desiring that we have a deep and intimate relationship with him.

Think back to a wedding you've attended, or perhaps your own wedding. We love to watch the groom as his beautifully adorned bride walks down the aisle to meet him. Each and every one of us is beautiful to the Lord in this very same way. But do we really understand that? Do we understand the relationship he desires from us? A young couple on their wedding day can't contain their excitement—not only for the wedding but also for the marriage that will last a lifetime! This is an I-can't-wait-to-hang-out-with-you kind of relationship, a relationship where I just have to pick up the phone and share all the exciting (and even boring) moments of the day with the one that I love. Two people in love want nothing more than to be together. That is the relationship God wants with each and every one of us, male and female alike.

Young love is fun, and our relationship with God should be too! But our relationship will mature over time. When I first met my husband, Chuck, I wanted to hang out with him all the time. I still do, but it's different now. When we get to hang out, we don't have to talk the whole time. Sometimes we just sit in silence. There's something comfortable, and comforting, about just being near him, to simply know he's there.

Prayer can be like this. We've made prayer so much about conversation that we forget it's mostly about communion. Learning this has been transformational in my life. Much of my prayer time nowadays happens in the mornings before I climb out of bed, when I'm still in a bit of a fog. This kind of communion started in my teenage years, after we moved from Germany to Kansas City. I had trouble sleeping at night because I would listen to the news broadcast, and daily there were reports of murders and shootings. Somehow the environment in which I lived, an American suburb, was terribly frightening to me. That might sound crazy, but I wasn't accustomed to American suburbs. I had been a city girl in Germany, and when we went to bed at night, the house was locked up tight. The shutters were closed over the windows, and no one would be able to get into the house. These American houses lacked security, and they frightened me. I would lie in bed at night listening to the darkness and wondering what murders were happening in Kansas City!

Some nights my mother would come in to pray with me and share different scriptures about the peacefulness of sleep that comes only from God. And then there was an overwhelming sense that Jesus was there in the room with me, guarding and protecting me, and I could go to sleep. It was the knowledge that the Lord was with me that allowed me to enjoy sweet and restful sleep. It was also this experience that brought me into a wonderful relationship with Jesus Christ, for I became accustomed to having conversations with him every night until I fell asleep. He was in the room with me, watching over me and caring for me. We would talk, and I would drift off.

Paul talked about praying continually (1 Thess. 5:17), but it didn't mean he was constantly peppering God with requests; it meant he was in constant communion with God. This kind of communion is not something that happens overnight, and it's a challenge in our busy world. There is much to keep us from slowing down and letting this actually happen. But God is there at the banqueting table, calling us to feast under his banner of love and allowing us to simply rest in his presence.

Give Up the List and Give In to Love

This kind of intimate love changes us. Gregory of Nyssa wrote a beautiful commentary on the Song of Solomon, saying that when we, as the Lord's disciples, allow ourselves to be vulnerable to him, we are wounded by the arrow of his love. Our hearts are suddenly opened by him and by the love that he wants to pour into us. Gregory says, "By a delicious wound she receives his special dart in her heart;

and then she herself becomes the arrow in the hand of the Bowman, who with his right hand draws the arrow near to himself, and with his left directs its head towards the heavenly goal."[2] "By being filled with the love of the bowman, her head is now turned heavenward, and the focus of all her attention becomes the bridegroom. No longer is transformation the goal; he is the goal."[3]

The late Dr. William Greathouse, one of my predecessors at Nazarene Theological Seminary, once told a story of a woman who had been married for a number of years. It was not a happy marriage. At some point, her husband had made a list of all the things he expected from her day after day. She adhered to his list, quite begrudgingly, because she didn't really receive anything from him in return. Eventually, her husband died, and a few years later, the woman remarried. Her new husband doted on her and showered her with love. One day, as the woman cleaned out a drawer, she found the list created by her late husband. Looking it over, she realized she did everything on that list for her new husband, simply in response to his love for her.

If we try to live by the list, we miss out. We grow frustrated and angry and hurt. But if we enter into a relationship with God and allow his arrow of love to wound our hearts, we will follow him because we love him, not because we've been told how we have to live. If I love God with all of my heart, then I want to be like him. I want to be near my beloved. If he's out on the streets and in the dark corners of the world, I have to go there because I love him, and there's no place I want to be but with him.

Loving God and loving neighbor—this is how John Wesley defined holiness. Our love for others, the love that propels us into the dark corners of the world where our beloved is, emanates from our love for God. In his book *The Church of Mercy*, Pope Francis compares this to the heart's movement of systole and diastole, its contraction and relaxation. It is in this movement that we find ourselves in "union with Christ" and in "encounter with others."[4] The contraction of the heart draws us toward Christ, and the relaxation of the heart reaches out to the world. If we do not have both beats, our hearts would cease to function.

If we are reflecting the Image, the heart is beating in systole and diastole, loving God and the world. One cannot exist without the other.

Discussion Questions

1. In what ways do you think the present-day church may be similar to the church in Corinth?

2. Talk about the difference between "luv" and God's love.

3. Can you think of examples of dim reflection in the church? In your own life?

4. Does an intimate relationship with God as portrayed in Song of Solomon make you uncomfortable? Why or why not?

5. How do you pray? Is it more conversation or more communion?

6. If we love God, we want to be near him. What are some of the "dark corners of the world" where he is that we must also go?

FOUR

REFLECTING LIGHT

We are called to reflect the Image, and Jesus is the Image. This requires a response from each of us. The Image is already there, but we need to face him in order to reflect him. We as humans have turned our backs on God. Even in the midst of our sin, however, God continues to turn toward us and reach out to those who are lost.

Psalm 67:1-2 says, "May God be gracious to us and bless us and make his face to shine upon us, . . . that your way may be known upon earth, your saving power among all nations." The prayer of the psalmist is for God's face to shine upon us—a representation of God's presence emanating from him, continually reaching out toward his beloved humanity. The psalmist cries out for God's grace to reach out to each and every single person.

But are we turned toward him? The only way that we can be a reflection of his face is for us to be facing him. In sin we turned away, and now we must take responsibility to respond to his grace, to turn around in repentance, lifting our faces to God our Father, the Creator of all things, and allow his face to shine upon us. What happens in that moment is a restoration of the relationship that God intended for all of humanity—one in which we are face-to-face and nose-to-nose with our God. This is only possible through Christ—the Image. The God of the Old Testament is almost dangerous for us, but when Christ comes, it becomes possible to see the face of God. His face shines on us, and the reflection seen within us is the glory of his majestic presence.

In another psalm, having found himself in a difficult circumstance, David offers these words:

I sought the LORD, and he answered me,
    and delivered me from all my fears.
Look to him, and be radiant;
    so your faces shall never be ashamed.
This poor soul cried, and was heard by the LORD,
    and was saved from every trouble.
The angel of the LORD encamps
    around those who fear him, and delivers them. (34:4-7)

Surrounded by an enemy, David sought the very face of God—he turned toward the God that he knew loved him and would care for him in the midst of his deepest need. As he looked to God, his face radiated with the glory of God's very presence.

David was a man who knew how to settle into God's holy presence, relaxing in the grace of God. Notice that David was not without problems! His life was filled with trouble and difficulties, but he knew how to call upon God, and then, even in the midst of his struggles, he was surrounded by God's holy presence.

Whenever we read about God's radiant glory, we know that he is present. Moses is the ultimate expression of this radiance when he returns from Mount Sinai with the commandments, his face glowing. The people were so disturbed that they asked him to wear a veil over his face (2 Cor. 3:13).

We see this radiance again in the New Testament, when Jesus takes Peter, James, and John to a high mountain. The gospel of Matthew tells us that "he was transfigured before them, and his face shone like the sun, and his clothes became dazzling white. Suddenly there appeared to them Moses and Elijah, talking with him" (Matt. 17:2-3). Jesus comes to earth as the visible image of the invisible God, and as the Image, he is also the Light. So if we are reflecting Christ, then we are reflecting the Light into the darkness of the world.

Before Christ came, God often revealed himself through fire, as he did in the tabernacle where Moses met with him. The tabernacle had no windows, so unless the fire of the altar of God was burning, the place was shrouded in darkness. In Numbers 8, God speaks to Moses and instructs the priests to light the way to the altar by arranging seven lamps in front of the lampstand. The lampstand was to be lit from the fire of the altar, and each of the seven lamps was to be lit from the lampstand.

The fire of the altar represents the Source of all light—God himself! But no longer do we need a tabernacle or temple. Jesus came to earth to be the Light for us, and by being in relationship with him, we receive our light directly from him. We are to take that light into the world to help to light more lights. In this way the light of Christ is taken beyond the Source and into the places of darkness. At the same time, our lights are to illuminate the path that leads to the

Source. People need the pathway lit so that they can find their way to Christ.

If the priests did not follow God's instructions to light the tabernacle, then the very light of God would not shine, and the path to the altar would not be found. If we do not follow the instructions of God in our own lives, there will be darkness in this world and people will not find their way to God. We have a responsibility to be the shining lights of God in this world, illuminating the pathway to God.

I remember long, dark winters in Russia. Moscow is as far north as Sitka, Alaska, so we similarly experienced long days in the summer—the sun might not set until midnight and might rise at 3:00 a.m.—and, conversely, very short days in the winter. I once watched a beautiful winter sunset, then looked at my clock and couldn't believe it was only 3:30 in the afternoon! During those short days, our children would leave for school in the dark and come home in the dark. I joked with them that someday they would be able to regale their children with tales of walking to school by moonlight when it was twenty-five below—and it would be true.

On the way home, we hoped the streetlamps would be working so we could make our way through the ice and snow. Generally, we carried a small flashlight to try to illuminate the path that others had created, following closely in their footsteps. Even when we arrived home, often there would not be light. Entering a dim hallway, we waited for our eyes to adjust before fumbling to the elevator or walking up a dark staircase. When trying to find someone else's home, we had to count each flight of stairs to determine when we had arrived on the right floor. There, we would be greeted by four darkened doors, sometimes with no numbers. Out came the flashlight once again in an effort to determine, there in the darkness, whether we had reached our destination. If we were lucky, a number was penciled in somewhere on a doorpost.

Our Moscow apartment building didn't have enough power for all the new electric appliances everyone wanted to use. At night the building gradually grew dim as more and more people arrived home from work and tried to share the power. So for years, we burned candles every night. I know how long tea lights last—four hours—because they would burn every evening from 6:00 to 10:00 p.m. in our apartment, enough time for dinner and homework. When they went out, it was time for bed. The darkness had come.

But, oh, the joy of a crisp, cold, sunny winter morning! The sun did not rise until after 9:00 a.m., but the brightness of that light changed the day. At times the darkness became normal to us, and not until the sun peeked over the horizon did we remember what we had been missing.

Uncomfortable Illumination

In the beginning was the Word, and the Word was with God, and the Word was God. He was in the beginning with God. All things came into being through him, and without him not one thing came into being. What has come into being in him was life, and the life was the light of all people. The light shines in the darkness, and the darkness did not overcome it. (John 1:1-5)

We try to comprehend the coming of our Lord and Savior, Jesus Christ. The reality is, at times, difficult to grasp. Humanity had fallen, and still is falling, into the depths of sin. The result is darkness. What happens when we are stuck in darkness? Sometimes we become accustomed to it, and we think that this is the normal state of things.

When God sent Jesus, the Light shone into the world, and it continues shining into our sin-darkened world today. But have we become accustomed to the darkness? Do we feel comfortable with the dimness, where we can hide away, hoping that no one sees our weaknesses? The gospel of John tells us that the world did not comprehend the light of Jesus when he came into this world in the flesh (1:10). How much more so today when we must accept the Light by faith!

The truth is, the radiance of God's presence can make people uncomfortable, including those who may call themselves followers of God. This was the case for the Israelites. When Moses went into the Tent of Meeting and up on Mount Sinai to receive the commandments, he sat in the very presence of God. Moses grew so close to God and spent so much time with God that he literally glowed. When he returned to the camp, his face shone with the reflection of God's glory (Exod. 34:29-35). The Israelites were afraid of what they saw reflected in the face of Moses. The awesomeness of the presence of God frightened them to the point that they asked Moses to put a veil over his face. Unlike Moses, they did not want to walk daily in a relationship with a holy God. Instead, they wanted to keep him at a "safe" distance.

What is it about reflecting the face of God that makes those around us uncomfortable? There is vulnerability involved in seeking God's face. We cannot hide in the shadows and seek him. We must be willing to come out of our own safe places and move toward God. People around us may think that we are strange because our behavior doesn't fit the mold of what we as humans have defined as the Christian walk. But who are we to define what the Christian walk looks like? The Christian walk is one in which we are seeking the face of God daily and allowing his reflection to shine on the world around us.

The Christian walk is a radical walk. It is not a comfortable, go-to-church-a-few-Sundays-a-month walk. Rather, it is a walk that is transformational to the core, in which we are willing to walk in obedience to the will of God as we seek his face. God has never been about challenging us to live a comfortable and satisfying life! God has always been about stretching our boundaries and continually drawing us toward a deeper walk with him that is transformational, both to ourselves and to the world around us. Instead of a comfortable life, it can be disturbing.

In his second letter to the Corinthians, Paul encourages the church in Corinth (and us) to not be afraid of God's presence:

Since, then, we have such a hope, we act with great boldness, not like Moses, who put a veil over his face to keep the people of Israel from gazing at the end of the glory that was being set aside. But their minds were hardened. Indeed, to this very day, when they hear the reading of the old covenant, that same veil is still there, since only in Christ is it set aside. Indeed, to this very day whenever Moses is read, a veil lies over their minds; but when one turns to the Lord, the veil is removed. Now the Lord is the Spirit, and where the Spirit of the Lord is, there is freedom. And all of us, with unveiled faces, seeing the glory of the Lord as though reflected in a mirror, are being transformed into the same image from one degree of glory to another; for this comes from the Lord, the Spirit. (2 Cor. 3:12-18)

A new day had dawned for the children of Israel, and for all of us. The veil can be removed for those who want to have a deeply intimate and personal relationship with God—just as Moses did! Moses had to go daily to the Tent of Meeting, but through the power of the Holy Spirit, we have the incredible privilege of meeting with the Lord daily. The Holy Spirit becomes a mediator that allows us to seek the face of God and to see his glory. Paul tells us here that we see the glory of God "as though reflected in a mirror" (v. 18), and the early church fathers often referred to us as the mirrors that can now reflect the glory of God to the world. And as mirrors, the closer that we are to the Image, the greater the reflection of Christ in our mirror. Thus if someone looks at us, he or she sees us as transformed into the image of Jesus Christ. And this relationship of drawing closer to Christ continues throughout our entire lives so that the transformation occurs "from one degree of glory to another" (v. 18). The work of the Holy Spirit draws us into this ever-transforming relationship in which we move from glory to glory in the power and presence of God. This is God's plan for his holy people.

The closer we draw to God, the more our lives become a reflection of God's grace and glory that shines light into the dark corners of other people's lives. This may make them feel uncomfortable—especially people who call themselves followers of God but don't want to go deeper in their walk with the Lord. Instead, they would prefer that we cover up so that they would not see God reflected in our behavior.

But our purpose in life is not to make other Christians comfortable. Our purpose is to clearly reflect the image of God to a needy world. That means that you and I must be in a right relationship with God so that we can reflect his glory to others. Then his way will be "known upon earth" and his "saving power among all nations" (Ps. 67:2). We become the living testimonies to the transformational grace and power of God, and the result is not that we are praised but that God is glorified in all the earth.

Can We Just Flip a Switch?

You are the light of the world. A city built on a hill cannot be hid. No one after lighting a lamp puts it under the bushel basket, but on the lampstand, and it gives light to all in the house. In the same way, let your light shine before others, so that they may see your good works and give glory to your Father in heaven. (Matt. 5:14-16)

Here again, in the Sermon on the Mount, Jesus talks about light and the fact that now *we* are the light! How do we become the light? The light is from God alone, and we must seek the face of God, which results in us becoming his light to the world. It is his radiant glory that lights up the world, and this is the light that no one can hide. Sadly, even those who call themselves Christ followers seem to be trying to make it alone these days. Taking the time necessary to seek the face of God seems to be inconvenient. Instead we want something that will be a little faster and easier. It was never fast or easy for Moses, David, or Jesus—why should it be for us?

We are not a people in need of new strategies for bringing people to Christ; we are a people who need to seek the face of God. It is his radiant glory that will attract people, not to us, but to him.

But what does this look like in our daily lives? If we were going skiing for the first time, we wouldn't hop onto the lift, ride all the way up, then effortlessly swoosh down. It takes time, practice, and lots of face-plants in the snow! I love to ski, and my husband does not—at all. I have tried and tried to teach him, and it has never worked. When we were in Russia, we sometimes traveled to our denomination's regional office in Switzerland, and I would take our daughters skiing. On one such trip, I thought that instead of trying (and failing) again to teach Chuck to ski, we could pay for an instructor. Imagine how thrilled he was with me when he spent the entire day going down a bunny hill with a group of little children! Ah, how he loves me and wanted to try. By the end of the day, however, he seemed to have mastered the hill, so I invited him to ski down the mountain with me. We went up only halfway, and when we exited the ski lift, he looked petrified. He glanced at me and said, "You know, I've never really figured out how to make myself turn." So I told him to just follow me, and I would take him down the hill slowly. But because he couldn't turn, he took off way too fast, and I had to yell after him to just throw himself down in the snow. Once he hit the ground, he took off his skis and said, "I'm walking the rest of the way down, and you're not getting me to go up that hill again. I'll come with you, read a book in the lodge, and drink hot chocolate, but I'm not going back up there again."

The view at the top of the mountain was breathtaking, and I wanted my husband to see it. I wanted him to experience how beautiful it was, but if he didn't know how to ski, he couldn't experience it. In the same way, God wants us, on our spiritual journey, to be on the climb, to reach the top of the mountain, and to look out with a bird's-eye view at the incredible beauty. God is inviting us into this kind of experience and relationship, and if we don't learn how to go up the mountain, we're going to miss out on it.

If we are going to be transformed from glory to glory, then there is the upward call that encourages us to continue the spiritual climb throughout our entire lives. The Holy Spirit is our Guide, but we must also put in some effort. This is why we often read about the need to practice spiritual disciplines. What does that look like in your life? For me it includes the discipline to be in the Scriptures every day that I can, and it includes time in prayer. It also includes situations where I have to step back and ask God for direction and guidance. It's sitting down on a plane and asking God whether he wants me to have an intentional conversation with the person next to me. It's the intentionality of being Jesus to the waiter or waitress I encounter today. It's praying for God to help me have "evangelism eyes" and see the people I meet today the way that he would see them. It's praying that I can be Jesus to my family today. It's praying that God helps me to know what I should say yes to and what I should say no to, and it's praying and studying for God's wisdom and leadership as I prepare sermons to present at different events and services. And that's probably just the tip of the iceberg.

Prayer is crucial to our transformation. The Rev. Kevin Myers, pastor of the Wesleyan 12Stone Church, tells the story of moving his family from Michigan to northern Atlanta because he believed God was calling him to plant a church there. He wanted to build a large and vibrant congregation, but the first few years, the services typically ran eighty people. Then he heard God tell him to give up his dream of a large church and start spending his Saturday nights in prayer with his congregation. "If you are present with me on Saturday nights, then I will be present with you on Sundays," was the promise God gave. Myers listened and obeyed, and a little more than a decade later, 12Stone has grown to fifteen thousand people.[1] God kept his promise—as the church spent time with him, God poured out his presence in their midst.

I don't know about you, but I want to join Moses on that journey into the very presence of God. I want to be transformed from glory to glory until the world no longer sees me but sees Jesus in me. There are days when I stumble and fall on this journey, but through the grace of God, may I be able to get back up, brush off the dirt, and continue the climb.

Walk in the Light

The people who sat in darkness
> have seen a great light,
and for those who sat in the region and shadow of death
> light has dawned. (Matt. 4:16)

The people who walked in darkness
> have seen a great light;
those who lived in a land of deep darkness—
> on them light has shined. (Isa. 9:2)

Jesus' life was the fulfillment of the words of the prophet Isaiah. The text in Matthew is a quotation from Isaiah but with a significant change: In Isaiah the people are walking in darkness and living in the land, but by the time Matthew brings us this word, the people are sitting in darkness and in the region. No longer are they seeking the face of God but instead have chosen to sit and to wallow in their ignorance.

What a huge difference between sitting and walking! Walking conjures up the imagery of those who are seeking God and actively engaged in the process. The ones who are sitting? They seem to have given up. This scripture suggests that the Israelites had become satisfied in their ignorance. Why bother with trying to get to know God? We'll just plunk down and live with what has been handed to us.

I'm afraid that too many of us are living in ignorance these days. Maybe it's been a long time since we've seen a movement of God's Holy Spirit in and among the lives of people, bringing about real spiritual transformation. Is it possible that is happening because we are sitting? I would like to suggest that God's people must become active in his work, walking and moving and constantly seeking his face.

Looking closely at the text, the people in Isaiah who were walking and living also had light shining on them. The light of God was able to transform their lives, and although they had lived in darkness, now life was illuminated. This was the promise of God. As Jesus appeared, so the Light would appear. To those who had given up all hope and had simply sat down in the darkness, the Light had dawned. God in his mercy has never given up on his people. He continues to seek out those who may be sitting in darkness without hope, and his light dawns on them. The Light is going into the dark corners of the world.

Now we can understand how we become active participants in God's work in the world. When the light of Jesus shines on us, we become reflections of his image. The way that the Light can shine on those sitting in darkness is for us to take that Light to them. The Light will find them in the dark places of this world when we unite with Christ in his work, reflecting the light of his image on those sitting in darkness.

What is our posture today? Are we among those who are sitting or those who are standing? If you have chosen to sit in the darkness, and the pain is more than you can bear, cry out to God for the Light to dawn on you and lead you out of darkness and into his light. This is his promise, to bring us out to safety. If you are walking today, then be a great reflection of the Light, allowing his light to shine into places where people are hurting and sitting in the darkness. Either way, it's time to take action; it's time to move closer to the One who came to show us the way back home and into the safety of his loving arms.

Do not be afraid to be a shining reflection of God's glory. Do not cover up what he wants to do in your life. Be a blinding reflection of the Light, and in doing so, you will be a living testimony to the world.

Discussion Questions

1. Can you think of an experience when uncomfortable light shined into your life?

2. What about the opposite? Has light from your life made someone else uncomfortable?

3. Do you welcome the Light into your life, or have you grown accustomed to the darkness? Are there places in your life you are trying to keep hidden from the Light?

4. How do we become the light? Do we just flip a switch?

5. What is your current posture? Are you sitting or walking?

FIVE

ABIDE, AND FRUIT HAPPENS

In John 15, we find Jesus saying, "If you abide in me, and my words abide in you, ask for whatever you wish, and it will be done for you. My Father is glorified by this, that you bear much fruit and become my disciples" (vv. 7-8). From this teaching, we could probably park on the word "abide" for about a month! Too often we jump right past it and get into what we assume is our business—bearing fruit. Or even going out to make "Christlike disciples in the nations."[1] But if we don't "abide," we miss the whole point. We turn the Christian life into a type of "works" for the kingdom.

The work is done by God—not by us. Our job is to abide in him. What does it mean to abide? Among its synonyms are "to stay," "to endure," "to reside," "to dwell," and "to remain." So first and foremost, we have to learn how to slow down, turn off the noise, and sit in his holy presence. There is nothing about rushing through a few devotional thoughts and saying grace at the table that equates to "abiding." To truly become reflections of Jesus Christ, we are going to have to spend time with him, and for most of us, it's going to take discipline—which, not surprisingly, is the root of discipleship—to develop a practice of dwelling in his holy presence through prayer.

In the Old Testament, abiding in the tent of the Lord was reserved for people who had developed a very personal relationship with God. The Tent of Meeting traveled with the children of Israel, and Moses spent time abiding in that tent, along with Joshua. The women who were the keepers of the entrance to the tent spent much of their lives tending to the tent. It was the sacred space where heaven and earth met, and those who entered it had come simply to be in the presence of the most holy God.

Therefore, in Psalm 15, the psalmist asks, "Who may abide in your tent?" (v. 1). It's a valid question because the tent was the very heart of fellowship with God, and yet it was a holy and sacred place. The good news of the psalm is that the tent was open to all who would live as God's holy people, and that included

Those who walk blamelessly, and do what is right,
    and speak the truth from their heart;
who do not slander with their tongue,
    and do no evil to their friends,
    nor take up a reproach against their neighbors;
in whose eyes the wicked are despised,
    but who honor those who fear the LORD;
who stand by their oath even to their hurt;
who do not lend money at interest,
    and do not take a bribe against the innocent. (Vv. 2-5)

This psalm was written before Christ came to earth, and yet there are parallels to the Christian life here. Who is invited into the tent? When the Messiah came, he destroyed the barriers, and all of humanity was invited into the Tent of Meeting. Now people of every race and nation, male and female, slave and free, are invited to enter and fellowship with God.

Do you imagine that Moses and Joshua were in and out of the tent in five minutes, getting their time with God crossed off their list and out of the way? Entering the tent does not mean dropping in and hurriedly leaving, but instead settling in and making this our place of dwelling. We make our home in the Lord. God becomes the very center and focus of all things, and all that we do is based on this relationship of abiding in his tent. When we emerge from the tent, our interaction with the world will be defined by our time in the tent. The behaviors listed by the psalmist are the result of spending time in the tent. When Moses spent time in the Tent of Meeting with God, the very glory of God began to radiate from him. When we spend time in God's presence, his very nature begins to be reflected in us and by our responses to the world around us. We do what is right, we speak truth, we do not slander, we do no evil, we honor those who fear the Lord, we don't lend money at interest, and we do not take bribes. The time in the tent changes the way we look at the world around us and the way we treat others.

God purposely brought his tent to us, through Jesus, so that we can enter into this sweet fellowship today and every day. The incarnate image of God came to this earth to draw his children to him. This was God's original plan for his creation—for humanity. This was when we could, for the first time, see God in human form, and at that moment we understood that we were to be in his likeness—by being a reflection of him. In this way Jesus bore fruit—reclaiming those who were called to be the holy people of God. When we abide in Christ, when we are transformed into his likeness, then not only do we look like him, but we also act like him and participate in his work. Through us, God's children are reclaimed and reunited with Christ. This is bearing fruit, and if you are truly a disciple, bearing fruit is not an option—it is the natural result of abiding in him. We don't bear fruit to become a disciple; instead, a disciple is someone who abides in Christ and, as a result, bears fruit—because Jesus bears fruit!

The Path of Good Works

We are constantly reminded that we are saved by faith and not by works. In Ephesians 2:8-9, Paul tells us, "For by grace you have been saved through faith, and this is not your own doing; it is the gift of God—not the result of works, so that no one may boast." These verses were part of the "Evangelism Explosion" years ago. The emphasis certainly is on the work of Christ in our salvation. We are not saved by our own works but by God's grace if, in faith, we are willing to receive this gift from God.

But right on the heels of this comes verse 10: "For we are what he has made us, created in Christ Jesus for good works, which God prepared beforehand to be our way of life." Once we have received this gift from God, we are once again God's beautiful creation, restored to the Image, which is God's intent for humanity.

What happens when we are restored and we reflect the original Image? We are restored for good works so that we can walk in them. God intended for good works to be a "way of life," a journey. Too often we have emphasized the "gift" and the "grace" of the moment of salvation and have overlooked the importance of the path of grace. This entire passage in Ephesians is more about the journey than the moment. Clearly, there is a moment of new birth, but if that becomes the only focus, we miss out on the richness of all that we learn here. Too many "Christians" are not experiencing what it means to be alive in Christ. We are trying to live in a moment—one which may have been a long time ago—and are not living in the journey. Christ died for the whole journey—to restore humanity. Yes, there was a moment, but it's really about the journey. It's about abiding.

This abiding life in Christ is a transformational life. We are to stop sinning! Why is that? Because when we are in Christ, we are restored to the creatures that God originally intended us to be. To be fully human means that we fully reflect the image of Christ, and Christ did not sin.

The idea of not sinning has been hard for Christians to accept because we are humans who live in a fallen world. How could God expect us to live without sin? The answer comes in 1 John 3, in which abiding becomes key to the writer's understanding of living without sin:

No one who abides in him sins; no one who sins has either seen him or known him. . . . Those who have been born of God do not sin, because God's seed abides in them; they cannot sin, because they have been born of God. . . .

. . . All who obey his commandments abide in him, and he abides in them. And by this we know that he abides in us, by the Spirit that he has given us. (Vv. 6, 9, 24)

On our own, we cannot live without sin. The writer reminds us that the "seed" of God abides in those who are born of God—and that means that when we are born again, God himself abides in us, and God cannot sin. It is those who "know" God on an intimate level who do not sin, but the possibility exists only because of the indwelling of the Holy Spirit.

Sadly, too many Christians want to give excuses for continuing to live in sin, usually saying something such as, "We're 'only human' and can't help but live this way." God's intention for humanity was to abide in him. To be truly human is not an excuse, because to be truly human is *not* to sin. It is the corruption of humanity that sins. God is calling us back into the original relationship he intended between humans and himself so that we may all become truly human again.

For the Cappadocian Fathers, sinful humanity was thought to be a corruption. Augustine had a different understanding. He believed that original sin was something stuck in us that we had to purge. This is problematic for our understanding of living a sinless life. But if we understand sinful flesh as a corruption, we know it's not a thing to get rid of; instead, we realize that we are people who need to be healed. Fallen humanity is more like sick humanity. When we start throwing around arguments that we have no choice but to sin because we are "only human," we have to ask ourselves, At what point do we really believe in God's power to heal the corruption in humanity?

From this perspective, Jesus Christ assumes human flesh and heals humanity through his life, death, and resurrection. Jesus' entire life is a moment-by-moment sanctifying of human flesh. He becomes the ultimate human and prepares a pathway for us so that we, too, can be healed. The image of God had been lost to humanity, but by Christ's assumption of humanity, he again restored the Image to humanity, making it again possible for us to reflect the Image.[2]

We're born corrupted, with all of these issues in life that we have to deal with, but God wants to draw us closer to him and bring healing to us. If we are constantly in relationship with Jesus Christ, we will find our healing. We are made fully human when we are in relationship to him, and he wants to bring healing and wholeness to us.

The secret to the Christian life is not to focus on trying to be righteous or to live free from sin but to learn to abide. And how do we abide? By turning toward God, by seeking his face day in and day out, by desiring to be as close to him as humanly possible. As a result, we are transformed into his image and likeness here on this earth! Too often when we read scripture about being sinless, we think that there is some kind of superhuman effort involved. It has nothing to do with me (except staying close to him) and everything to do with him. If I am abiding in him, when people look at me, they don't see a sinner; they see Jesus who lived without sin. We seem to get this wrong, imagining that we can follow a list of rules and therefore be without sin. The key is to abide, and abiding means that Christ is *in* us and *he* is the one who is without sin. The more that he consumes us, the more of his nature is in us, and we do not sin.

This is possible only through the indwelling of the Holy Spirit. It became obvious that humans could not walk this journey by simply following the rules of the Old Testament. Jesus had to live, die, be raised again, and return to heaven so that the Holy Spirit could come and live in each one of his followers.

The life of the transformed Christian is one in which we do good works, not because we want to be saved, but because we *are* saved. Our lives after coming to Christ should be ones in which we no longer do the things that we did in the past. God says we are to walk in good works. Now that is certainly a challenge, to ask God to keep us in such a close daily relationship with him that we are able to walk in *his* good works! Remember, this is not about human effort but about a relationship with God in which we remain in such close contact— abiding with him—that we walk the journey of life he has laid out for us, which leads us on a path of good works.

Have You Had Your Bath?

The abiding life is God's intent for humanity. Throughout Scripture, he is revealing himself to us and inviting us into this intimate relationship with him. In the Old Testament, for instance, the story line is ever pointing to it.

Then he made the molten sea; it was round, ten cubits from rim to rim, and five cubits high. A line of thirty cubits would encircle it completely. Under it were panels all round, each of ten cubits, surrounding the sea; there were two rows of panels, cast when it was cast. It stood on twelve oxen, three facing north, three facing west, three facing south, and three facing east; the sea was set on them. The hindquarters of each were toward the inside. Its thickness was a handbreadth; its rim was made like the rim of a cup, like the flower of a lily; it held three thousand baths. He also made ten basins in which to wash, and set five on the right side, and five on the left. In these they were to rinse what was used for the burnt offering. The sea was for the priests to wash in. (2 Chron. 4:2-6)

Solomon, as he builds the temple of the Lord, includes a "molten [or cast] sea" that would cleanse the priests before they offered sacrifices to God on behalf of the people. The sea was a large bronze bowl holding three thousand "baths" of water, the equivalent of eighteen thousand gallons or sixty-six thousand liters—the size of the average backyard swimming pool.

A few years ago while in ancient Ephesus (modern-day Turkey), I was walking through the ruins of a church. There, in what would have been a holy room behind the altar, was a very large basin sitting on a pedestal. When I read about the cast sea in Solomon's temple, I pictured this large basin. It was not as large as this sea described in 2 Chronicles, and yet it was quite significant in size. This basin in the city of Ephesus was used for baptism. Could there be a connection between the cast sea and the baptismal basin?

The sea in Solomon's temple was created for the priests' use alone. It is believed that the bowl itself held the water but that water poured out of the bowl as a type of fountain, and the priests cleansed themselves in the fountain's stream. Only after being purified by the water could they go into the very presence of God, placing sacrifices before him. Some historians believe that the sea's panels included depictions of the Ten Commandments, symbolizing the purification of the law of God and a reminder that the cleansing of the priests also came with obedience to the law of God.

That cast sea no longer exists, and neither does Solomon's temple. Jesus said that the temple would be destroyed but that he would raise it up again in three days (see John 2:19-21). We know now that he was referring to himself and that he is the living Temple! No longer does a priest have to make sacrifices for us; we are now invited into the "priesthood of all believers." We don't need an intermediary because we can have a personal relationship with Christ.

If we are all priests, then it would make sense that we are all invited into this symbolic cleansing. The sea is replaced with the baptismal font, and instead of the priests being cleansed, we are the ones made clean. Instead of stepping into a fountain of water, we step into the fountain of the Holy Spirit, who washes away the filth of our lives and leaves us pure in the presence of God. Instead of the Ten Commandments written on the walls of the sea, they are written on our hearts. This is the sign of the new covenant. The old has passed away, and all things are made new (see 2 Cor. 5:17).

Sadly, some of us are still trying to make our way to God through the old system. We are trying to follow the legalism of the past without wanting to step into the bath ourselves. It seems easier if we don't have to get wet—let someone else do it for us! But Jesus has called us to jump into the deep end, to be filled with his Holy Spirit and be bathed in his presence day in and day out.

The result of this daily soak is that our lives will overflow with love for God and love for others. That is what those who have been through the bath do! Their lives genuinely reflect a change. They become living panels of the Ten Commandments, and the world sees Jesus in them.

It is through this abiding relationship that we draw closer to the image of God, Christ. In doing so, we become a clearer reflection of who he is, for we are students who reflect the Master from whom we are learning. Fourth-century mirrors that the Cappadocian Fathers used were polished metal, like those in Paul's day. They didn't understand reflection the way we do. In their ancient Greek understanding, the reflection was much more than skin deep. A mirror didn't simply reflect an image but took on the qualities of what it was reflecting. For them, reflection represented a real change, almost to the point that the image facing the mirror became burned onto the mirror itself.

That must be true for us as well. To be a reflection of the Image, we need to be genuinely changed. The closer we get to Christ, the more we actually take on the qualities of the Image that we are reflecting; his image actually becomes a part of who we are.

Can you imagine an entire mass of people being reflections of Christ in this world? In his writings, Dionysius of Alexandria told about a plague epidemic that struck his city in 226. A mass exodus took place as people fled from the disease. But most of the Christians stayed. Even as family members left their dying in the city, the Christians remained to care for the sick. They brought them food and medicine, comforted them, and nursed them—knowing full well that they could catch the disease and die with them. Many did. "This Christian generosity," wrote Dionysius, "seemed little short of martyrdom itself."[3] Their actions became a real turning point in Christianity. Family members of those who had died were so moved because of what they saw in the people who came to be known as the Martyrs of the Plague of Alexandria.

What the people of Alexandria saw was Jesus reflected in his followers who were, no doubt, abiding in him. When we abide in him, we take on the qualities of the Image that we are reflecting. We bear his fruit. Abiding changes us and, consequently, changes the world.

Discussion Questions

1. How do you spend "time in the tent"?

2. Read Ephesians 2:8-10 again. Are you familiar with verses 8-9? What about verse 10? Why is it important to read these verses together?

3. How is it possible for us to live without sin?

4. Do you often hear the phrase "only human" in religious circles? Do you think about it differently after reading this chapter?

5. How does God heal our corrupted flesh?

SIX

THE "PERFECT" ONES

What does a life of love look like? Scripture gives us so many examples of God's love. In the Sermon on the Mount, Jesus illustrates a new kingdom in which the love of God rules all things. He sits down with the crowds and lays out a blueprint of how this kingdom would operate on a completely different plan than earthly kingdoms.

You have heard that it was said, "You shall love your neighbor and hate your enemy." But I say to you, Love your enemies and pray for those who persecute you, so that you may be children of your Father in heaven; for he makes his sun rise on the evil and on the good, and sends rain on the righteous and on the unrighteous. For if you love those who love you, what reward do you have? Do not even the tax collectors do the same? And if you greet only your brothers and sisters, what more are you doing than others? Do not even the Gentiles do the same? Be perfect, therefore, as your heavenly Father is perfect. (Matt. 5:43-48)

The final paragraph of Matthew 5 is all about relationships. God's people were proud that they at least loved their neighbors but kept their distance from their enemies. Jesus was going to change all of that. He told them to love their enemies. He said that in his kingdom, it is our responsibility to love those who don't love us. Why? Because we are to be perfect.

How we hate hearing the word "perfect"! Why? Because in our understanding of the word, we will never get there. We mess up, we get mad at our spouses and kids, and so on. The idea of a perfect human being who never makes a mistake and never errs in anything he or she does can drive us all crazy because we know that we can never reach that level of perfection.

Yet right here in the Sermon on the Mount, Jesus calls us to be perfect.

Paul also uses the word "perfect" over and over when he describes the Christian life. However, every time he uses the word, he simultaneously instructs us to press on, such as in this passage:

Not that I have already obtained this or have already reached the goal; but I press on to make it my own, because Christ Jesus has made me his own. Beloved, I do not consider that I have made it my own; but this one thing I do: forgetting what lies behind and straining forward to what lies ahead, I press on toward the goal for the prize of the heavenly call of God in Christ Jesus. Let those of us then who are mature be of the same mind; and if you think differently about anything, this too God will reveal to you. Only let us hold fast to what we have attained. (Phil. 3:12-16)

How can we already be perfect and still need to keep moving toward something more? What we have to remember is that Paul's understanding of perfection and the twenty-first-century Western understanding of perfection are two radically different ideas. Paul's (and Jesus') Jewish-Greek understanding of perfection was that the created vessel would fulfill the purpose for which it was created. The trouble with most of us English speakers is that we don't always understand the world of the original Greek writers and their use of a word such as *teteleiōken* (he has perfected). Whenever we see the word "perfect" in the Bible, we can assume that we will find the Greek word *telos* as its root. *Telos* can mean "end," "goal," or "completion," and so *Teleioō*, the verb form, means "I reach the goal" or "I bring to completion." In other words, we complete (*teleioumen*) the purpose for which we were created. That purpose is to become a reflection of the Image.

For by one sacrifice he has made perfect forever those who are being made holy. (Heb. 10:14, NIV)

For by a single offering he has perfected for all time those who are sanctified. (10:14, NRSV)

Here again we find the Greek root *telos*, and using a Greek understanding of "perfect," this scripture tells us that Christ, by sacrificing his life, has brought to completion "those who are being made holy," or "those who are sanctified."

"Holiness," "sanctification," "perfection"—pause for a moment and examine your reaction to these three words. They might be the Bermuda Triangle of Christian terminology, propelling us into a vortex of frustration. Many people hate these words because they carry with them some negative connotations. Sadly, it is self-described "holy" and "sanctified" people who have tended to give the words a bad reputation. Among those who call themselves "holiness" people are some of the most unhappy and downright mean people I have ever met. When folks in the world see this and say that they don't want anything to do with the church, can we blame them? They look at us and say, "Oh, you're the ones who think you can be perfect." But that's because we have allowed the true concept of these words to be misconstrued. We have made them all about us, and we have discovered that on our own, we cannot measure up. That is true! If we think that we can become sanctified or make ourselves holy or perfect by following a list of dos and don'ts, then we are wrong.

There is something to be learned about dependency upon God, and this comes as we continue this journey. This includes our understanding of holiness, for we do not make ourselves holy. Holiness is revealed in our lives only as we have greater dependence upon Jesus Christ.

The writer to the Hebrews says that Christ's sacrifice made it possible for the image of God to be restored in humankind. This restoration was the perfection—or the completion—of humanity. John Wesley in his *Explanatory Notes upon the New Testament* describes this as Christ having "done all that was needful in order to their full reconciliation with God."[1] In other words, Jesus Christ provided everything necessary in his life, death, and resurrection for complete and total reconciliation with God. Because of Christ, humans could fulfill the purpose for which they had been created: they could be a reflection of their holy God. By daily turning their faces toward God, humans would be sanctified by God's ongoing and continuous holy presence.

Let's examine the relationship between "holiness," "sanctification," and "perfection," since these words have been, at times, misconstrued. "Holiness" has to do with the very nature of God, and based on our understanding of the relationship within the Holy Trinity, the nature of God is holy love. God's intention for all of humanity is for us to be included in that relationship so that when we are adopted into the family of God, we are made holy. "Sanctification," in turn, is both a momentary event and an ongoing process by which we are made God's holy children.

We can apply the mirror imagery here. When our mirrors are turned in the wrong direction, they are not reflecting the Image. The prodigal son, similarly, discovered the consequences of turning his back on his father and going his own way. He found himself in a pigpen, wishing he could go home. But in the son's father we find likened the grace of our heavenly Father. Standing on the side of the road, the father never stops looking in the direction of his son. Likewise, our heavenly Father never turns his back on us but instead, in grace, continues looking in our direction, constantly calling us back to him and giving us all we need to respond to his call. It is then, through the Father's grace, that we respond and are again placed in a right relationship with the Image. We reflect the Image because we are turned in his direction.

There is, however, a problem. We are still far away. While living in sin, our mirrors became covered with the dirt that sin brings with it. The grace of God continues to draw us nearer to the Image, but the dirt obscures the reflection. To be a true reflection of the Image there must be a moment when we are made clean so that the reflection can be complete. But even after this happens, there must be an ongoing cleansing and movement toward the Image. Just as we have to clean our own homes, so our spiritual homes need to be kept clean by the power of the Holy Spirit, and we must continue moving toward the Image because even if we are turned toward Christ, considering the distance, the reflection may be awfully small! For Christ to completely fill our lives (and our mirrors), we are constantly drawn and compelled to move toward him.

This leads us to the word "perfection." If perfection means we fulfill the purpose for which we are created, and our purpose is to be God's holy people, then perfection and sanctification become one and the same. As God's sanctified child, each of us is reflecting the perfect image of Christ. Notice the action verb "reflecting." This is an ongoing and active process, which means that we should in turn also understand perfection as "perfecting."

It's an action! It's what is happening in our lives—an active verb of being and becoming what God intends for us to be. Let's read Hebrews 10:14 again:

For by a single offering he has perfected for all time those who are sanctified. (NRSV)

For by one sacrifice he has made perfect forever those who are being made holy. (NIV)

The word "sanctified" in the *New Revised Standard Version* is translated "being made holy" in the *New International Version*. Why is that? Because the verb tense of the word connotes a continuous, active process. Jesus' work of perfection was once and for all, but the act of sanctification is ongoing—perfecting.

Holiness Is Not Optional

Holiness, sanctification, and perfection are God's intention for everyone. For Christians, those of us who have been adopted into the family, this is not optional. But it's not about me doing everything right; it's about me being a reflection of Christ. We have taken it to mean that we don't make mistakes, and that has created a number of paranoid Christians. There's this idea that if I go to church today and down to an altar to reconcile with God, and then I make a mistake tonight, I'm going to hell. We live in fear of that hell. We have gone down this whole path of "name it and claim it" theology, but if we claim to be holy and sanctified, what do we do with the fact that we've got issues and we're messed up? We talk about sinless perfection, but that has been a major roadblock for confession because we have tried to claim perfection in the wrong sense—so much so that we've created an environment for emotionally unhealthy individuals who cannot be honest about the issues in their own lives. They reason that if they are perfect, confessing they have need of God's help in areas of life where they are struggling must mean they are not perfect or holy or sanctified. What this boils down to is that we live in a petrified state of ugliness because we don't believe that we ought to confess anything.

John Wesley didn't see it that way. He practiced confession almost weekly. He and the other "methodists," nicknamed for their methods or practices, formed what were called classes and bands. These were small groups who met to confess sin, which Wesley defined as "a voluntary transgression of a known law of God,"[2] and to confess what he called "infirmities."[3] Wesley understood that it would take accountability to help us in our relationship with God. Living a holy life is a pretty serious, deep commitment, but again, it's not about a list of rules; it's about living the life. Wesley talked about holiness as "love excluding sin."[4] Our love for Christ becomes so great that there is no room for sin in our lives. It's about what we do—love—rather than what we don't do.

Where we run into trouble is failing to understand holiness, perfection, and sanctification as relational. If we're not abiding in Christ, then we create our own image of Christ and reflect it. We make it this list of dos and don'ts, and we reflect the list. We make ourselves and our own moral activity the focus instead of the reflection of Christ in us. It's been very destructive to our own self-esteem because we think we can never measure up. The "perfection" the world calls us to is a distraction from all that God is calling us to be. Likewise, we have made sanctification something that it is not, and the result is that we have written it off as unattainable. In the meantime, I'm afraid, we have become satisfied with a mediocre faith that is not transformational. We believe that we are being humble when we say that there is no way that we can be holy or sanctified while here on this earth. That's not humility; it's a lack of faith and trust in the very nature of God. The reality is that we have few people seeking this deeper transformational walk with Jesus Christ because we enjoy running our own lives.

In some ways, the list is easier. We want the Christian life to be a list because we can live with the list. We just want to know what we're supposed to do and not supposed to do in order to be holy, sanctified, and perfect, and secure our ticket to heaven. It's not that cut-and-dried, though, because it's about a relationship. We are all mirrors reflecting the same Image, but each of our frames is a bit different.

I once preached a message in a small holiness church in Ohio. This church was founded in 1908, and I was told it is the oldest church of its denomination east of the Mississippi river. Just above the spot where I was preaching hung a sign that read, "Holiness unto the Lord." When that church was founded a little over a hundred years ago, this was likely the war cry of the congregation. Those old-time holiness people really believed that the power of the Holy Spirit was transformational, even for the dirtiest down-and-out sinners. They believed it so much so that they made signs and plaques and sewed banners that read, "Holiness unto the Lord." They hung them around their church buildings and even wore and carried them in parades!

Do we believe holiness is optional, or do we believe it is possible? Many of the churches have removed those old signs that read "Holiness unto the Lord," thinking that the phrase sounds old-fashioned and irrelevant today. But maybe they've simply forgotten what that sign really stood for and the incredible message borne therein!

We cut ourselves short if we don't realize that the hope of holiness is not only available for all of us but also God's desire for each of us. The question is whether we are willing to go on to that deeper walk with him, letting go of the things that tie us to this world. Only then does his sanctifying grace wash over us and make us a clean mirror with no streaks—one that can perfectly reflect his holiness.

We Are the Saints

This idea of a sanctified Christian is not new. In the early church, every follower of Jesus Christ was being sanctified. In his letters,

Paul would refer to the "saints" in the different cities. But how do we define "saints"? We think of people like Mother Teresa and put sainthood so far out there that it's not attainable for ordinary people. This is not the case. For Paul, saints were the people of God in whom the Image had been restored, so now they were God's holy people. These are the sanctified. These are the saints. Once our orientation is again toward God, we are, and will be, sanctified because of the reflection of God's holy nature—love—in our lives.

So it is God whose holy nature is love and who has done the work of perfection, but sanctification, the process of perfecting, also is dependent upon our continuous and active role. Consider the beautiful prayer of Jesus in the gospel of John before his crucifixion: "Sanctify them in the truth; your word is truth. As you have sent me into the world, so I have sent them into the world. And for their sakes I sanctify myself, so that they also may be sanctified in truth" (John 17:17-19).

The word "sanctify" has a dual meaning here; it means that Jesus' desire was for his disciples to be made holy, and this was an act of God. But it also was Jesus' prayer that they be consecrated, or set aside, for the special calling they had received from Jesus. He prayed this prayer in the garden of Gethsemane, just a few hours before he would die on a cross. He knew that the disciples would soon be set aside to be his representatives in the world until the day they died. His prayer was for them to consecrate themselves wholeheartedly to God, be made holy by God, and be sent into the world, again by God, to do his work. Jesus knew that none of this would be possible without his action, for the disciples could only be a reflection of him and his holiness. Therefore, he sanctified himself; he set himself aside and was consecrating himself, ready to enter the holy of holies as the ultimate sacrificial Lamb so that the hope of holiness would be possible for all of those who would become a reflection of him.

But there is some action required on our parts in our sanctification. We must have a purposeful desire to participate in the holiness of Jesus Christ. Jesus wasn't just praying for the disciples who were present in the garden more than two thousand years ago; he was praying for you and for me. And his prayer was that we be sanctified. Perfection, sanctification, holiness—none of these are optional, second-act benefits of being a follower of Jesus Christ. God's original plan for all of his children is to be his holy children! Why? Because we are to be a reflection of Jesus—and Jesus is holy.

Just as Jesus had to wrestle with his entire consecration to the task before him, could it be possible that we, too, must wrestle with our entire consecration? Jesus prayed and asked his Father to take the cup from him. He didn't want to have to go through the day ahead—it was going to be awful! But as he prayed and sweat drops of blood, he came to the place where he was able to give it all up in obedience to his Father. For us, it may be with great tears and sweat that we struggle to give up our future to God. But just as Jesus had to go through this moment in his own life, so we have to go through times in our lives when we must determine whether or not to move forward in the truth.

Reflect Christ and Imitate Christ

To be in a sanctifying relationship with God, we must face him daily. If not, we will no longer reflect him and his holiness. Our journey of sanctification takes us closer and closer to him. If you are standing fifty feet from a mirror, and you move toward the mirror until you are five feet away, what happens? Your image doesn't change, but the size of it does. We have to move closer to God, and the closer we are, the greater his reflection will be in us. Having been made perfect—turning toward God and being restored in the image of God—the perfect reflection of Jesus is evident in our lives.

There is a difference in reflecting Christ and imitating Christ. Paul tells the Corinthians, "Be imitators of me, as I am of Christ" (1 Cor. 11:1). Imitation of Christ is our grace-enabled human participation in this process. If we want to look like Christ, maybe we ought to put a little effort into it. If Christ spent time in prayer with the Father, maybe we should. Hopefully, we reach a point where we can't distinguish the difference between our imitation of Christ and the reflection of the Image in our lives. The church fathers believed in a synergy that happens in a human imitating Christ and a human reflecting Christ. This is not a works theology because it's not about being saved; it's about putting our effort into imitating Christ after being saved. Imitation is our effort, albeit assisted by the Holy Spirit; reflection is his. It's our activity combined with his activity that draws us closer to him.

We, as Paul did, are to "press on toward the goal" (Phil. 3:14), which is Jesus Christ. We keep seeking his face, turning in his direction and straining toward him.

> Therefore, since we are surrounded by so great a cloud of witnesses, let us also lay aside every weight and the sin that clings so closely, and let us run with perseverance the race that is set before us, looking to Jesus the pioneer and perfecter of our faith, who for the sake of the joy that was set before him endured the cross, disregarding its shame, and has taken his seat at the right hand of the throne of God. (Heb. 12:1-2)

The finish line of this race is not something that exists here on this earth, but instead the goal of the entire race is Jesus Christ. The word "looking" in Greek means to turn from looking at anything else and now to look only at Jesus. Why? Because he is the "pioneer" (v. 2)—but that word means so much more. He is the Captain, the Team Leader, and also the Coach, but not only that—he is the one who built the racecourse. Who else would know the way but the One who created the path? So stop looking anywhere else and look only at Jesus.

But he is more than just the "pioneer" who created the course; he also is the "perfecter of our faith" (v. 2), and once again, we find the Greek root *telos*. So he is the one who brings the whole race to completion. Jesus is the Creator of the course, but the course leads to him. The goal is to become like him and to unite with him. Jesus endured the cross, but that was not the goal. He endured the cross so that now he can be seated "at the right hand of the throne of God" (v. 2). And our invitation is to this very place with him.

Even good religious things can keep us from keeping our eyes on Jesus and from the goal. I stress this because for years in my own life, I never heard Jesus brought into the message of holiness. Too often the message of holiness seemed to focus more on me and my behavior, and the course laid out before me, I believe, claimed most of my attention. I worried about how to make it through the obstacle course of life, wanting to run my lap well, but without looking to Jesus.

We should never, ever stop or slow the journey of drawing closer to God, which is our continuous, ongoing sanctification. Every follower of Jesus Christ is called to a deeper walk with him—to be made holy. In other words, the "normal" state for every believer should be holiness. We have twisted that terminology to describe a select few who are special, and yet it truly is the desire of God for every one of his followers.

When humanity fell, we lost what God had intended our relationship with him to be. For humans, to be made perfect or "truly human" is to have the image of God restored in us, because that is the purpose for which we were created—to be a reflection of Jesus Christ to the world. Having been made perfect, having been restored in the image of God, the perfect reflection of Jesus is evident in our lives, but this is just a part of the journey. Paul was never satisfied that he had "made it" but instead constantly kept his face turned toward the goal, which was Christ himself. This, too, must be the goal for our lives—to never stop climbing, to never stop growing, to never stop being transformed, to daily seek the glory of the Lord and his holy presence in our lives, to reflect and to imitate.

The *Telos* Is Love

Guess where else we find the word *telos* in Scripture? The famous love chapter. "Love never ends. But as for prophecies, they will come to an end; as for tongues, they will cease; as for knowledge, it will come to an end. For we know only in part, and we prophesy only in part; but when the complete [*teleion*] comes, the partial will come to an end" (1 Cor. 13:8-10).

No wonder this chapter becomes the climax of Paul's letter to the Corinthians! He refers to the fact that when we are children, we have the characteristics of children. We speak, think, and reason like children (see v. 11). But when we grow up, we change—and the same is true spiritually! We are never to be staying in the same place spiritually but always to be growing and maturing. There are things that we don't understand at this point and time in our journey, but the goal is none other than God himself, and if we continue to face in his direction, the closer that we get to him, the clearer he will become.

If we become focused on the wrong things, we will be drawn away from the goal or *telos* of all humankind, which is love. That's exactly what Paul wanted the Corinthians to understand, and it's important for us today as well. Too often in the church we have become so focused on externals—on our own personal holiness (if there can actually be such a thing)—that we have drifted along with the Corinthians. We need to be reminded that there is only one goal or purpose in life, and that is to get to know God. God's passions become our passions, God's heart becomes our heart, and we are driven by our desire for him. When we fall deeply in love with God, we also fall deeply in love with the world that he created. His desires for all of creation become our desires for all of creation, and our daily lives are driven by God's desires. That is why everything else becomes fleeting in the light of the depths of our personal relationship with him. All these other things—prophecies, tongues, knowledge—can become a distraction to truly knowing God's love. This is the goal. There is nothing better than love, because love is God.

No, I don't like the word "perfect" because it conjures up the wrong picture in my mind, but Jesus *is* perfect in all ways. For me to be perfect is for him to shine through me—Jesus, the perfect One!

Therefore it's not impossible to be made perfect in this lifetime. We are to fulfill the purpose for which we were created. We are to reflect the perfect One to this world that so desperately needs to see Jesus. And we are to never stop the spiritual journey—we are to be ever growing and drawing closer to him. Gregory of Nyssa actually said that he thought it was a sin to *not* be growing spiritually. That is our calling, as God's people, to take responsibility to keep facing the right direction and keep climbing toward Jesus!

That's why there is always a relational aspect to sin. When we sin, or when others sin, relationships are damaged. First of all, as a result of sin, our relationship is damaged with God the Father. When we are in a right relationship with him, we are facing him, and when we are facing him, our lives become a reflection of him to the world around us. For this to happen, we must repent of our sins, turn around, and begin to move toward the *telos* of our lives, which is Christ. In doing so, we are in relationship with him, and we become a reflection of him and his nature to the world around us.

The second result of sin is broken relationships with others. Adam and Eve sinned, and their relationship with God changed, but so did their relationship with one another. No longer were they equal partners working in the garden, but Eve was to serve Adam. This was not God's *telos* for humanity but the result of sin and corrupted relationships. Jesus came to say that these relationships are again to be set right because of the new kingdom, the one in which we are to be perfect—a perfect reflection of God. And if we are to be a reflection of the perfect relationships *in* God, what does that look like? Remember, God, in the Holy Trinity, is an incredible relationship of pure and holy love, where the Father loves the Son, and the Son loves the Holy Spirit, who loves the Son, who loves the Father, and so on and so forth. This is what is to be reflected in each and every one of us! If God constantly reaches out to sinful humanity, always and forever trying to draw us back into a relationship with him, shouldn't this also be our response to a sinful world around us? That is, if we are in a right relationship with him!

It's important for us to remember that the call to the life of sanctification and perfection is for those of us who have turned to face Christ. When Paul wrote letters to the churches, he did not tell the believers to go and make the pagans stop doing what they were doing; he told the believers to not participate in what the pagans were doing. It is in God's nature to reach out and to love the unlovable, and so that is to be our nature as well. Only in this way will we be partakers of the new kingdom together with him.

God, through his prevenient grace, is constantly reaching out to humanity in a desire to draw humans back into relationship with him. Since humanity has free will and can choose whether to respond to God's act of grace, those to whom we reach out can also choose whether or not to respond. However, the response of another is not our responsibility. We must simply continue to reach out and never give up! It's what Jesus would do.

Is the kingdom of God reflected in our relationships with others? This is the call of Christ to each and every single one of us: "Be perfect, therefore, as your heavenly Father is perfect" (Matt. 5:48).

Discussion Questions

1. What connotations does the word "perfect" have in your life?

2. How is it possible for us to be perfect? Talk about the Greek word *telos* and how it is different from our modern-day definition of "perfect."

3. What images and definitions do you associate with "holiness" and "sanctification"?

4. Is confession something you see practiced in your church? Is it something you practice in your life? Why or why not?

5. Talk about the difference between reflecting Christ and imitating Christ.

6. Does understanding sin relationally change your perspective on sin?

SEVEN

LOVE GOD, LOVE EACH OTHER— AND PASS IT ON

Growing up in the church, I was reminded often that my body was the temple of the Holy Spirit, and therefore, I should take care of my spiritual body. If you, too, grew up in a holiness church, you may be familiar with the admonition: "Don't drink, smoke, chew, or go with those who do." (Interestingly, no one ever wanted to talk about eating and physical exercise as ways to care for the body as a temple—but that's another topic.)

When my family lived in Idaho, my gym class was coming up on a square-dancing segment, and I must have mentioned this to my mother. She forbade me to participate and sent a note to school asking for me to be excused from the exercises for religious reasons. I was so embarrassed. I had to sit along the wall and watch my friends square-dance, and I thought, "What is wrong with what they're doing?" I remember going home and asking this question. It wasn't that my mother necessarily thought dancing was evil. She was the pastor's wife, so she didn't have much choice in these types of situations. One day she and I watched a musical on television, and she declared, "I don't think there's anything wrong with that kind of dancing."

I needed to find answers to my questions—not just, "We don't do that." I needed to understand *why* we don't. In my readings about John Wesley, I learned that his views on dancing had to do with not wanting to exclude the poor. Balls in eighteenth-century England were society events (think of any Jane Austen book), so dancing was another division between the rich and poor. This made sense to me.

Maybe we've misunderstood the temple of the Holy Spirit. So often in my early years, the communal aspect of the temple was completely overlooked. The entire focus was upon me as an individual taking care of my personal temple. That's what was stressed whenever we read this scripture: "Do you not know that you are God's temple and that God's Spirit dwells in you? If anyone destroys God's temple, God will destroy that person. For God's temple is holy, and you are that temple" (1 Cor. 3:16-17).

The *New International Version*'s translation gives a better understanding of the plural form of "you" in this text: "Don't you know that you yourselves are God's temple and that *God's Spirit dwells in your midst*? If anyone destroys God's temple, God will destroy that person; for God's temple is sacred, and *you together are that temple*" (emphasis mine).

"You together are that temple." Doesn't it seem that this scripture is instructing us to live out the Christian life in community? Think about it: God in the Trinity is a community bound together by holy love. We are to be a reflection of God to the world, and if God is communal, then our reflection of God also should be communal.

This is difficult to grasp when we have painted a picture of the Christian life as something incredibly individualistic. I think I would question, however, whether it's possible to be a Christian without being relational. Jesus, in a nutshell, commanded us to "love God" and "love our neighbor." Both of those are very relational commands. I am not the temple; instead, the community of faith unites to become the temple in which the Holy Spirit dwells.

Jesus also told us that "where two or three are gathered in my name, I am there among them" (Matt. 18:20). Isn't that interesting? He described his presence within a community of faith. So instead of an individualistic path to faith, it is within the community of faith that we can be shaped and molded into the people of God. It's not just me, God, and my TV (or, these days, my webcast of my favorite church service). Just like the Corinthians, there may be times when we want to run from the community out of frustration. However, we must realize that even with its warts, bumps, and bruises, the community is where we can learn to be God's holy people. We are intended for community—for the church—if we are to be true reflections of Christ.

A Prostitute's Declaration of Faith

The Old Testament story of Rahab has always fascinated me. She belonged to one community but was drawn toward the community of faith, and her decision to change loyalties altered the course of history.

Rahab was labeled a prostitute. More than likely, she ran the local inn, where travelers from out of town would stay. It wasn't uncommon that in these types of places, certain "comforts" were provided. It was simply the culture of the day. However, this woman was unusual because she had heard about—and believed—the stories of the God of the Israelites.

Then Joshua son of Nun sent two men secretly from Shittim as spies, saying, "Go, view the land, especially Jericho." So they went, and entered the house of a prostitute whose name was Rahab, and spent the night there. The king of Jericho was told, "Some Israelites have come here tonight to search out the land." Then the king of Jericho sent orders to Rahab, "Bring out the men who have come to you, who entered your house, for they have come only to search out the whole land." But the woman took the two men and hid them. Then she said, "True, the men came to me, but I did not know where they came from. And when it was time to close the gate at dark, the men went out. Where the men went I do not know. Pursue them quickly, for you can overtake them." She had, however, brought them up to the roof and hidden them with the stalks of flax that she had laid out on the roof. So the men pursued them on the way to the Jordan as far as the fords. As soon as the pursuers had gone out, the gate was shut.

Before they went to sleep, she came up to them on the roof and said to the men: "I know that the Lord has given you the land, and that dread of you has fallen on us, and that all the inhabitants of the land melt in fear before you. For we have heard how the Lord dried up the water of the Red Sea before you when you came out of Egypt, and what you did to the two kings of the Amorites that were beyond the Jordan, to Sihon and Og, whom you utterly destroyed. As soon as we heard it, our hearts melted, and there was no courage left in any of us because of you. The Lord your God is indeed God in heaven above and on earth below." (Josh. 2:1-11)

This is quite a declaration for Rahab to make to the Israelite spies: "The Lord your God is indeed God in heaven above and on earth below." What's interesting is that Rahab typically is remembered for three things: (1) being a prostitute, (2) lying, and (3) being saved by the Israelites. Overall, her only redemption is that she is saved by the Israelites. But isn't there much more to the story? Why is it that we find her mentioned three times in the New Testament?

> By faith Rahab the prostitute did not perish with those who were disobedient, because she had received the spies in peace. (Heb. 11:31)

> Likewise, was not Rahab the prostitute also justified by works when she welcomed the messengers and sent them out by another road? (James 2:25)

Is it possible that the way we view things within our own human context is often not the way God views things in the kingdom? God's goal for all of humanity is that humans become transformed into his image—that humans become a reflection of him in this world. That trumps everything else. Rahab is remembered in Hebrews, not because she was a prostitute, but because she was a woman of great faith. Think of unfaithful Israel: How many times did the Israelites turn their backs on God? How often were they told that they were to worship God and him alone? They were instructed to remind themselves day in and day out that "the LORD [their] God, the LORD is one" (Deut. 6:4-9, NIV). The chosen people of God often failed in this regard, but this woman, Rahab, had incredible faith and believed that the Lord was God. She feared him and was willing to sacrifice all to serve him. Her faith in God surpassed her fear of the local authorities. That day, she changed loyalties and no longer was in service to her local government, but instead to God's kingdom. That's why she protected the spies' location—she was working for God!

Where else do we find Rahab? In the genealogy of Jesus Christ: "and Salmon the father of Boaz by Rahab, and Boaz the father of Obed by Ruth, and Obed the father of Jesse" (Matt. 1:5). Maybe we need to realize that we are creating our own rating system of sin. Because everything in the West is very individualized, we have made faith in God a very singular thing—our "personal" relationship with God, our "personal daily walk" with him—and have therefore made sin a very "personal" thing too. We tend to see obedience to God in personal terms but fail to see our corporate responsibility. When Rahab switched sides, she became part of the corporate body of the Israelites. She became part of God's people, and her responsibility to care for the whole was more important than caring only for herself. That's why she had to cover for the spies. In God's economy, all of us are interrelated and interconnected. Our behaviors, choices, and actions affect our entire community.

Rahab got it right. She saw the big picture and was willing to pay the price, and she is remembered throughout history as a woman of great faith—so much so that the Messiah came from her very root.

"They Will Know Us by Our Angry Blogs"

Let's jump back to 1 Corinthians 3:

According to the grace of God given to me, like a skilled master builder I laid a foundation, and someone else is building on it. Each builder must choose with care how to build on it. For no one can lay any foundation other than the one that has been laid; that foundation is Jesus Christ. Now if anyone builds on the foundation with gold, silver, precious stones, wood, hay, straw— the work of each builder will become visible, for the Day will disclose it, because it will be revealed with fire, and the fire will test what sort of work each has done. If what has been built on the foundation survives, the builder will receive a reward. If the work is burned up, the builder will suffer loss; the builder will be saved, but only as through fire.

Do you not know that you are God's temple and that God's Spirit dwells in you? If anyone destroys God's temple, God will destroy that person. For God's temple is holy, and you [together] are that temple. (Vv. 10-17)

Once again, Paul stresses how important it is for the faith community to be united. In this passage, he addresses the Corinthians' argument over human leadership and whom they would follow. Loyalties were divided within the body of Christ. Somehow they didn't understand that this division was exactly what the enemy desired. There is nothing better for our enemy than to mutilate the body of Christ into tiny, ineffective pieces.

To help the Corinthians understand this better, Paul began to talk about God's temple. He didn't mean the temple in Jerusalem but a new temple made up of living stones. Each and every single member of the body of Christ is one of those stones, and each one has a purpose in the temple. This new temple is the church, the bride of Christ, made up of humans united in their faith and bound together by the power of the Holy Spirit. Jesus laid the foundation, preparing the way for everything that has come after to be built upon him. Every one of us, all of us who have come after, are corporately working together to expand his kingdom here on this earth. Woe to us if we are too concerned about the personal nature of our faith and are unwilling to understand our responsibility as building blocks within the entire kingdom! When the fire comes, the tough times, our work built of shoddy materials will burn up, leaving holes in the temple of the Holy Spirit.

A pastor in Canton, Ohio, effectively illustrated this one Sunday morning when I visited. He started his sermon by telling the community about the support available through the church's small groups, and while he spoke, he took what looked like giant Legos and began to build. In the process, someone strode onto the platform, knocked all the blocks onto the floor, and walked away. The pastor explained that there are times in our lives when we are trying to accomplish things, trying to get our act together, and the enemy comes by and knocks all of that down. As he finished his sermon, he asked the church's small-group and Sunday school leaders to come to the platform, stand in a circle, and join hands. We'd all forgotten about the blocks by this time, until he stood in the center of the circle and began building again. The same guy came running up to the platform, but this time he couldn't get past the small-group leaders standing around the pastor. So often we think we can do this thing alone, but when we become part of a community, there are times the community has to do battle for us and protect us.

It's sad to say that persecution doesn't always come from the outside. Sometimes the battles take place within the church. Why would that be? Because not all who call themselves "Christians" are indeed Christ followers. Our world is filled with people who claim to be Christian but do not abide in Christ. These people often are the harshest toward true Christ followers. They create great disturbances within the church because they perceive the church as existing to serve them rather than understand the church as the bride of Christ that exists to serve God in the kingdom. At the hands of such "Christians," I have observed followers of Jesus Christ suffer persecution within the very walls of a church. And yet I have also watched saints emerge from the fallout as those persecuted have responded with gentleness and reverence.

I recently read an article titled "They Will Know Us by Our Angry Blogs."[1] How sad is that! It seems as if this age of social media has brought us to a place where we find it easy to aim darts at one another from the comfort of our living-room recliners. In my denominational tradition, our founders preached that the church should be a "broad tent." We were taught, first and foremost, "In essentials, unity; in nonessentials, liberty; in all things, charity."[2] (Of course, I've witnessed many an argument over our definition of "essentials.")

In Romans 14, Paul tells the believers that practices such as eating and holidays are not the essentials of the Christian faith. He instructs them to "welcome those who are weak in faith, but not for the purpose of quarreling over opinions" (v. 1). Paul's use of the word "weak" here is an affirmation that there are stages to our spiritual growth—something that we need to remember. Those who are new in their faith may be weak, and we must be careful that those who may be "stronger" don't destroy the faith of the "weak" by imposing their own understandings on the "weak" when they may not be ready for them.

I once heard a story about a church trying to reach out to its community after the neighborhood around the church had changed dramatically. The teens in the neighborhood were rough and disrespectful, yet the church was doing all that it could to love these young people and show them Jesus Christ. One man in the church, however, was terribly disturbed that one of these teens would not remove his hat when entering the church. The man literally became obsessed with that hat. How could this young person be so disrespectful and think that he could worship God if he kept his hat on! The man was ready to do battle over the hat rather than fight for the spiritual state of the young man.

These days, we may not be arguing over the same things as the Romans did, but we have found a wealth of new arguments that divide us. At some point we have to ask ourselves, are we simply enjoying the quarrel, or is this really essential to our faith? We need to remember that we, the church, are a broad tent. In my tradition, the original broad tent included people from the North and the South soon after the Civil War. Political positions were put aside as people joined hands in love for God and love of neighbor. Quarreling over political opinions was not acceptable within the tent. Instead, those in the broad tent focused on what they believed they could do together for God. And when this happened, they reached out and helped to change their world.

We must stop arguing over inconsequential issues and begin living as the broad tent, or temple, that God intended to be transformational in the world. God's temple is sacred—so much so that Paul gave a warning in 1 Corinthians 3: Don't destroy the temple! The temple, the community of faith, the church, the bride of Christ—she is sacred. I would echo Paul: "Do you not know that you are God's temple, . . . and you [together] are that temple?" (vv. 16-17). What a beautiful picture of God's desire for community among his people!

God Is Sanctified Through Us

In Ezekiel 39:27 we find these curious words: "When I bring them back from the peoples and gather them from the lands of their enemies, then I shall be sanctified through them in the sight of the many nations" (NASB). For God to be sanctified through us may seem a bit odd because we know that God is holy—it is his very nature—and he is not in need of sanctification. However, the world's perception of God derives from what it sees in his people. The *New Revised Standard Version* translates "I shall be sanctified through them" as "[I] through them have displayed my holiness." God is not viewed as a holy God if his people are not viewed as a holy people. When God's people act and respond in ways that are not in line with God's character, the people of the world assume that this is God's character being revealed.

These words from the prophet Ezekiel were spoken to the Israelites while they were in exile. They had long ago given up holy living and had given themselves over to so many foreign gods that no one even knew who the true God was anymore. God spoke through his prophet so that when the Israelites returned home from exile, they would be worshippers of him alone—and by doing this, God would again be seen as a holy God. He would be sanctified because they would reflect God as he truly is.

Is God sanctified through our responses, or are we reflecting some sort of a personal god to the world who in no way resembles the true holy God? We do not simply speak for ourselves. We must recognize that the world will connect us to the label we wear. Our actions and behaviors do have consequences, and not just for us individually: They become a reflection of the God whom we purport to serve and represent. For so many years, we have measured our faith by our own personal acts of piety. The people of my tradition are known as "holiness" people. We have been preaching for more than a hundred years about being "entirely sanctified" and being "cleansed," but unfortunately, somewhere along the way, the message began to describe a change in exteriors, such as what clothes women wear, whether they can wear earrings and makeup, and so on, and we became hung up on the outside. Jesus condemned the Pharisees for the same behavior long ago:

> Now you Pharisees clean the outside of the cup and of the dish, but inside you are full of greed and wickedness. You fools! Did not the one who made the outside make the inside also? So give for alms those things that are within; and see, everything will be clean for you. (Luke 11:39*b*-41)

Because we, too, often define holiness as the things we don't do, we fail to have conversations about what is at the root of the don'ts. And somehow it has led to the idea that to be God's holy people, we are not to engage with the world—that holiness is somehow about personal holiness and nothing more. The Pharisees had been hung up on the very same issues—cleaning the cup on the outside and yet not concerning themselves with what was on the inside. Jesus told them a complete cleansing resulted in a change from the inside out, which would become visible in ministry to the poor.

Why are governments around the world taking up the responsibility of caring for the poor? Could it be because they are filling the void that has been left by too many Christians who have been cleaned on the outside but have not allowed the Holy Spirit to so fill them that they become generous to the poor? The early "holiness" people firmly believed in the connection between holiness and ministry to the poor and the oppressed. Out of the holiness movement came the women's suffrage movement, the Salvation Army, Compassion International, and World Vision. These Christians engaged with the world in ways that people had never seen.

Early holiness leader Jonnie Jernigan spent much of her life "hunting out" unwed mothers and their children who had been shunned by the rest of the world. "I wanted to go to the low and the outcast, to those that no one else cared for, and tell them of a Savior that died for them," wrote Jonnie Jernigan in her early twentieth-century book of testimonies. "I wanted to go into the hovels of poverty and tell them of the Man of Sorrows, who had no place to lay his head, nor money to pay his tax, who was born in a stable and cradled in an ox trough, who through his poverty made many rich."[3]

What has happened to us today? Have we become too "respectable" to work in these areas?

A few years ago, a shooting took place across the street from a church in Fort Wayne, Indiana, riddling a house with more than thirty bullet holes. The congregation could have decided to move the church somewhere safer, but instead, that church declared "enough is enough" and decided to stay. They united their faith with love and went out into the neighborhood to patch up bullet holes, clean up places where criminals hung out, improve lighting, and do whatever else they could to help care for that community. The reaction was overwhelming. Soon after, the church hosted a meeting where 250 Christians from a number of denominations gathered to join hands and pledge to be voices and advocates for an entire neighborhood. In the midst of it all, the community is seeing Jesus in action. The entire city is seeing Jesus in action.

Our actions, both in our individual lives and in our churches, reveal whether or not we are reflecting Christ. So we have to ask ourselves, "What do our actions say about our faith?" If we wear the label "Christian," what about our responses reflect the God whom we serve? It is a sobering reality, a huge responsibility to think that the reflection of God seen in us is the way that the world will perceive God. If God's people are not sanctified, will the world see God as holy? As followers of Jesus Christ, we have a responsibility to reflect the true God to this world as clearly as possible. Therefore, we must allow God to sanctify us and to fill us with his Spirit; we must allow his thoughts to become our thoughts. We must seek him with all our hearts so that the world may see the true God and that he may be a sanctified God through the actions of his people.

Anything short of this becomes a distortion of the Image. The Image is holy, and so the reflection should also be holy.

Leftover Pieces of Holy Men

Our actions impact those not only outside the church but inside the church as well. When the young people of today look at us and examine our lifestyles, do they see God reflected? They want to see genuine lived-out faith in community. If they do not see us practicing what we preach—or more importantly, practicing what Jesus preached—they will not buy into our faith. We've all heard the adages: "God doesn't have any grandchildren," and "The church is only one generation away from extinction." Perhaps these have become cliché, but we could use some sober reflection on them. The reality is that we *are* just one generation away from extinction, and I believe that we are seeing this come to fruition with lightning speed in the West. This is not a new problem; it is one that the people of God have faced time and again throughout history.

One attempt to curb this problem is found in Exodus 16: "And Moses said to Aaron, 'Take a jar, and put an omer of manna in it, and place it before the LORD, to be kept throughout your generations'" (v. 33).

As God led the children of Israel, he provided them with all that they needed for forty years. Six days a week, they stepped outside their homes and found fresh bread from God lying on the ground. All they had to do was collect it and eat it. On the sixth day they collected enough for two days so that they could rest on the seventh day. The manna really was a magical food! It must have had all the nutrients necessary to sustain human life, for it sustained this entire community of people year after year. It was so special that God instructed Moses to save some and store it in a jar to show to future generations so that they, too, could witness this miracle of God.

Moses did what God asked, but somewhere along the way, the people lost it. Not only did they lose the jar of manna, but they also lost the faith that should have been handed down. The people who witnessed and tasted of God's daily provision failed to pass on that faith to the next generation. Even so, God continued to be faithful to his children and, through Jesus, provided them with a promise for the future. Jesus had told them to wait for a new type of manna that would fall from heaven. His followers weren't sure what they were waiting for, but they went to Jerusalem and spent ten days in a prayer meeting until finally the new manna—the Holy Spirit—fell from heaven (Acts 1:12-14; 2:1-4). Peter stood up and preached a message to which thousands responded, receiving the gift of the Holy Spirit (2:14-42). No longer did God's miracle have to be saved in a jar for future generations, because all future generations would have the possibility of experiencing the miracle of God daily through the Holy Spirit.

I've visited numerous ancient churches in my lifetime, and it's amazing to me how many different "leftover" pieces of holy men are out there. If you put together all the pieces of Moses claimed by churches, you'd probably have a man with twenty toes and fifteen fingers! Not to mention the vast collections of hair. Who can say where all these pieces have come from, but they sit in churches, encased in glass, as a reminder of the holy men who have gone before us. A friend of mine tells the story of visiting a church in Damascus that claims to have the skull of John the Baptist. He had recently visited another church that also claimed to have John the Baptist's skull, and when he asked about this, he was told, "Oh, that's the one from his childhood. We have the adult skull." He couldn't contain his incredulous laughter.

Holy relics have righteous intent. These items have been saved for future generations so that we will remember the great ones who have gone before and be inspired to also be followers of God. However, there is a sad similarity among these churches: all of these buildings are rather cold and empty. There is no sense of the presence of God in these places. Instead, they mostly resemble museums, places to imagine the past.

Having a jarful of manna wasn't enough to convince the children of Israel to stay true to their faith. They could see it and could hear the stories, but unless they engaged in a relationship with God, it didn't mean anything to them. Therefore, God found a way to allow them to experience him every single day of their lives: he sent the Holy Spirit. This became the way God enters into communion with humans daily. No longer would people have to look to the events of the past—they could commune with God in the here and now!

We have the choice to engage our faith in these two ways: either we can be enamored with the old and try to keep the faith from being contaminated by placing it under glass, or we can engage in communion with God. One will leave us cold and empty, with very little to pass on to future generations. The other will breathe life into us, transforming us and making our faith desirable to others. This relationship will challenge us to be engaged with our world in new and different ways—never the same "way we've always done it"—so that others, too, can experience transformation. We have to avoid the temptation to hole up within our community and retreat from the world.

We live in a day and age where some are declaring the church's demise. I would like to affirm with the great sixteenth-century reformer Theodore Beza that the church "is an anvil which has worn out many hammers."[4] She continues to endure blows, but as the hammers attack, instead of the church breaking, the hammers break. Today she is enduring blows from the hammer of post-Christendom, and I'm tired of hearing people talk about the end of the church. At the end of the story, "the Spirit and the bride say, 'Come'" (Rev. 22:17). The church, with all of her warts and wrinkles, is the way God has chosen to work in the world. She's imperfect, yes, but if you're writing off the church, you don't have a very good ecclesiology.

The church has survived, and she will continue to do so. We ought to heed the words of Paul and not look for the temple's destruction (1 Cor. 3:17) but instead unite within the community of faith as the temple that breathes the breath of the risen Christ into a very hurting and needy world.

Pass It On

Jesus lays this out clearly in the parable of the ten pounds:

As they were listening to this, he went on to tell a parable, because he was near Jerusalem, and because they supposed that the kingdom of God was to appear immediately. So he said, "A nobleman went to a distant country to get royal power for himself and then return. He summoned ten of his slaves, and gave them ten pounds, and said to them, 'Do business with these until I come back.' But the citizens of his country hated him and sent a delegation after him, saying, 'We do not want this man to rule over us.' When he returned, having received royal power, he ordered these slaves, to whom he had given the money, to be summoned so that he might find out what they had gained by trading. The first came forward and said, 'Lord, your pound has made ten more pounds.' He said to him, 'Well done, good slave! Because you have been trustworthy in a very small thing, take charge of ten cities.' Then the second came, saying, 'Lord, your pound has made five pounds.' He said to him, 'And you, rule over five cities.' Then the other came, saying, 'Lord, here is your pound. I wrapped it up in a piece of cloth, for I was afraid of you, because you are a harsh man; you take what you did not deposit, and reap what you did not sow.' He said to him, 'I will judge you by your own words, you wicked slave! You knew, did you, that I was a harsh man, taking what I did not deposit and reaping what I did not sow? Why then did you not put my money into the bank? Then when I returned, I could have collected it with interest.' He said to the bystanders, 'Take the pound from him and give it to the one who has ten pounds.' (And they said to him, 'Lord, he has ten pounds!') 'I tell you, to all those who have, more will be given; but from those who have nothing, even what they have will be taken away. But as for these enemies of mine who did not want me to be king over them—bring them here and slaughter them in my presence.'"

After he had said this, he went on ahead, going up to Jerusalem. (Luke 19:11-28)

In this parable Jesus gives a clear picture of God's kingdom. The people listening to him assumed he was going to march into Jerusalem that very day and take over the city. They were ready for the kingdom of God to be a political power, overthrowing the current authorities and taking control. Jesus was trying to tell the crowds, and us as well, that the kingdom of God would transcend earthly powers and authorities. Jesus began the rule and power of the kingdom with his death and resurrection; however, the kingdom will not come to completion until his return. In the meantime, his servants working within the kingdom are to care for it and work to expand it. The Master would know whom he could trust with his resources. To some, much would be given, and to others, very little. Those with much would take the resources and work hard to expand the kingdom and become responsible for more and more within the kingdom. But there also would be those servants who would hear the good news, receive their pounds, and do nothing. They literally would take God's resources, wrap them up, and hide them away so they could not be "damaged." The Master did not want his resources to simply be protected—he wanted them used.

I wandered through Barnes & Noble recently, perusing the shelves. In the Christianity section, one subject obviously popular with readers is end-time prophecy. (These titles are similar to much of the literature found in the religion section of Barnes & Noble, in my opinion: they reveal what popular Christian culture "likes" but do not necessarily reflect the best stuff available to help us on our journey toward Christ.) My struggle with the sheer volume of material on end-time prophecy is that it seems to propagate attitudes much like that of the third slave in the parable of the pounds. Books on this topic shift our focus toward protection and survival. Isn't that what the third slave did with his money? Didn't he wrap it in a piece of cloth—protect it—and refuse to share it with anyone else? When we are consumed with our own protection and survival, we do not focus on the expansion of the kingdom. Instead, we become concerned with the encroachment of the world into the kingdom, and so we pull back, we protect, and we hope and pray that Jesus will soon return!

God's followers are not supposed to sit back and be protective of what they have, but they are to be active "doers" within his kingdom work. There is great encouragement in this seemingly strange word from the Lord. The days in which Jesus lived were extremely difficult for God's followers, and yet Jesus suggests in this story that not only could they live out a life of faith in the kingdom, but if they used the resources given to them by God, they also could work to expand the kingdom. When we join him in praying "thy kingdom come," we are not praying for a someday thing; we are praying for his kingdom to come today!

We may need to step back and reevaluate the resources that we have been given and examine how they can be used to expand the kingdom. There are hurting and needy people out there today who need to experience Jesus and the touch of the kingdom of God in their lives. Will we reflect Jesus to them? Will we use God's resources to touch them? Or are we waiting around in "safe mode" for the return of Jesus Christ, clutching on to what we have been given with all our might, not willing to reveal the treasure we have?

We, as God's people, are called to be a reflection of Jesus Christ to this world. And when we, together, are the mirrors, what a difference it can make! Think of the palaces of old, with their mirrored walls. I once visited the palace ballroom in Saint Petersburg, Russia, which is covered in mirrors from floor to ceiling. In the days before electricity, candelabras lit this vast room for royal parties. The parties could last only as long as the candles burned, usually somewhere between four and six hours. Before such an affair, the candelabras would be lowered to the floor and filled with candles. When raised to the ceiling, the candles shone light into the room, and the mirrored walls reflected that light, multiplying the impact of the candles. The room would be ablaze with light!

We, together, can be that kind of reflection. He is the Light. We are the mirrors. If we are facing toward him, drawing near to him, then the reflection of his light will shine into the dark corners of our world.

Discussion Questions

1. What dos and don'ts have you questioned? Are there any you are questioning now? Talk about them in the context of communal life.

2. What do you think it means to live our lives as Christians within the community? What are our "corporate responsibilities"?

3. What are the essentials of our faith? The nonessentials? What did Paul have to say about it?

4. How can we recover the practices of the early holiness people to care for the poor?

5. Can you think of things we might do in the church because "we've always done it that way"?

6. Where do you fall on the spectrum of protecting God's resources and passing them on?

NOTES

Chapter 3

1. Marvin H. Pope, *Song of Songs,* The Anchor Bible (New York: Doubleday, 1977), 19.

2. Gregory of Nyssa, *From Glory to Glory: Texts from Gregory of Nyssa's Mystical Writings,* comp. Jean Daniélou and trans. and ed. Herbert Musurillo (Crestwood, NY: St. Vladimir's Seminary Press, 2001), 198.

3. Carla Sunberg, "The Cappadocian Mothers: Deification Exemplified in the Writings of Basil, Gregory and Gregory" (PhD diss., University of Manchester, 2012), 153.

4. Pope Francis, *The Church of Mercy* (London: Darton, Longman and Todd, 2014), 17.

Chapter 4

1. Kevin Myers, presentation given at District Superintendent Leadership Development Program (DSLDP), September 2014.

Chapter 5

1. "Mission," Church of the Nazarene, accessed May 18, 2015, http://nazarene.org/mission.

2. Sunberg, "Cappadocian Mothers," 70.

3. Peter R. S. Milward, "Dionysius," in *Apostles and Martyrs* (Leominster, UK: Gracewing, 1997), 115.

Chapter 6

1. John Wesley, *Explanatory Notes upon the New Testament* (London: Thomas Cordeux, 1813), 2:277; comment on Heb. 10:14.

2. John Wesley, letter to Elizabeth Bennis, June 16, 1772, in *The Works of John Wesley,* ed. Thomas Jackson, 3rd ed. (London: Wesleyan Methodist Book Room, 1872; repr., Kansas City: Beacon Hill Press of Kansas City, 1986), 12:394, hereafter cited as *Works.*

3. Wesley, journal entry, July 24, 1761, in *Works,* 3:68-69; Wesley, Sermon 76, "On Perfection," in *Works,* 6:412-13.

4. Wesley, Sermon 43, "The Scripture Way of Salvation," in *Works,* 6:46.

Chapter 7

1. Karen Swallow Prior, "They Will Know Us by Our Angry Blogs," Her.meneutics, *Christianity Today*, May 2013, http://www.christianitytoday.com/women/2013/may/they-will-know-us-by-our-angry-blogs.html?paging=off.

2. Attributed to Peter Meiderlin. See *Wikipedia*, s.v. "Rupertus Meldenius," accessed February 20, 2015, http://en.wikipedia.org/wiki/Rupertus_Meldenius.

3. Jonnie Jernigan, *Redeemed through the Blood*, presented as a gift to Northwest Nazarene College, September 1920 (n.d.; Holiness Data Ministry, 1997), 5, http://wesley.nnu.edu/wesleyctr/books/0501-0600/HDM0530.pdf.

4. Theodore Beza, quoted in Owen Chadwick, *The Reformation*, Penguin History of the Church (1972; repr., London: Penguin Books, 1990), 159.